D1605950

More Haunted Tennessee

A New Collection of
Spine-Chilling Ghost and Monster Tales
from the Volunteer State

Charles Edwin Price

Drawings and Graphics
by the Author

The Overmountain Press
JOHNSON CITY, TENNESSEE

The reader will find some references to the Work Progress Administration's Federal Writers' Project from 1936-1940. These stories have been included as they were originally published, with minor editing changes for clarity.

For

Kayla McGrady

A grand storyteller in her own write!

Other books by Charles Edwin Price

Danger Train
The Day They Hung the Elephant
Demon in the Woods
Diggin' up Bones
Haints, Witches, and Boogers
Haunted Jonesborough
Haunted Tennessee
I'd Rather Have a Talking Frog
The Infamous Bell Witch of Tennessee
Lullaby Aggie of Sweet Potato Cave
The Mystery of Ghostly Vera
Something Evil Lurks in the Woods

Contents

Introduction

If memory serves, the first time I laid eyes on Ed Price was in Abingdon, Virginia. My family and I were there for a brief vacation, and Ed was there to sign books. Whether we actually met and talked at that point, I don't recall. But it was the first of many times that my path and Ed's crossed. As often as not, those path-crossings happened to be book signing events in which we both took part.

I've sat beside Ed through many such signing sessions, and more than once, I admit, have felt a certain envy at the number of readers who stop by to pick up whatever happens to be his latest book. But I've never been surprised at his popularity. What Ed Price writes is engaging stuff. Pick up an Ed Price book, read one of his typically brief, fast-paced chapters, and odds are good you'll read at least one or two more of them—maybe five or six more—before you put the book down. And be assured that the book won't remain idle for long. You'll go back to it again—just once, because that second sitting will take you through to the end of it.

What accounts for the appeal of Ed Price's stories? I could note that the stories are educational—which they are—or that the folklore they preserve is too important to be lost—which it is—but the truth is actually far simpler: Ed's work is appealing because Ed's work is fun. Folklore, after all, only becomes folklore because it catches something universal, something that intrigues. And Ed knows how to retain that quality in his own retellings.

One of the things I appreciate much about Ed Price is the attitude he takes toward his work. Ed doesn't just collect stories because he needs them as grist for his literary mill. Ed recognizes that folklore is of inherent value...and most importantly, that folklore isn't only something that formed a long time ago, like rock formations in some musty old cave. Rather, folklore is living, ongoing, forming all around us, every day. Due to our modern communications technology in fact—the Internet in particular—it's growing faster, spreading faster, than ever before in human history. Ever heard of the urban legend?

In Ed's latest book, *More Haunted Tennessee*, he returns to one of his most familiar and popular literary territories: the ghost story. It's a genre that Ed handles deftly. One of the reasons he does so, I believe, is that he comprehends what ghost stories are all about better than most...or perhaps what they are not about. He doesn't waste much time on the question of whether a particular ghost tale is "true" or not.

Because truth isn't the point. The point is the shivery tale itself, and the universal fears, excitements, and questions that it evokes. I've read several of Ed's ghost story volumes and recommend *More Haunted Tennessee* as one of the best. If you're a Tennessean, you'll particularly enjoy it, but this is not a merely regional book by any stretch. It may be Ed's most broadly based, broadly appealing work yet, and I for one hope it finds an audience that spreads across the nation.

There are good stories in these pages, well told, sometimes mystifying, sometimes frightening, and often funny. If you're an established Ed Price fan, as I am, you'll find plenty here of what you've already come to enjoy. If you're a first-time Ed Price reader, then congratulations. You've picked a good point of entry for a fine body of work.

Welcome to *More Haunted Tennessee*. You'll find it a very worthwhile, very thrilling, very fun ride. Just don't read the really scary ones too late at night.

Cameron Judd
February 1999

Preface

You say that you don't fear the night—the time when mysterious shadows cast the world into a pit of darkness? You say that mysterious sounds coming from something you can't see don't make your heart beat faster or cause a cold sweat to break out on your forehead? Consider yourself fortunate. Some people never get over their fear of the dark, or of the mysterious shadows that continually swirl around us, or of the ghosts who visit us in the middle of the night.

Some people go all through their lives without seeing a single ghost, but some see spooks on a regular basis. These people are sometimes called sensitives because they are "sensitive" to the supernatural. Most of us, to be on the safe side, like to visit only with the ghosts of our imaginations. If you are one of the latter, then this book is for you.

This volume contains thirty bone-rattling stories about night creatures, boogers, and other assorted denizens of the Tennessee netherworld. Tales of giant fish, floating ghosts, headless ghosts, benevolent ghosts, vengeful ghosts, and ghosts that foretell the future eddy like swirling mist from these pages. Here you will find tales of pranksters whose ghostly tricks backfire, horrible creatures protecting buried treasure, and terrifying specters lurking in mirrors. By popular request I have even included a "Jack tale" in this collection.

Some of the tales are "true" stories—accounts of personal experiences with the supernatural. Others are yarns that have been passed down through the generations. Still others fall into the category of tall tales with a mystical tone. I have also added more than the usual number of humorous stories, just to keep things in perspective.

Ghost tales are world travelers. The motifs (the dominant theme or central idea) of these stories are by no means exclusive to Tennessee. For every story of a ghost that guards a Tennessee treasure, you will find like stories of a ghost that guards a New Hampshire treasure, a California treasure, or a Bavarian treasure. And for every headless spook that ranges in Tennessee, there are hundreds of other headless spooks scattered around the country—all behaving in practically the same way. Stories travel with the people who tell them, and the folklore of one area is spread to another like scattering seeds in the wind.

Folktales are not limited to the boundaries of any geographical region. A good example of this universality is the "Rap... Rap... Rap" story in this book. Over the past ten years, I suppose, I have heard this same story told in a hundred different areas of Tennessee, Virginia, or North Carolina. The theme of the tale always remains the same. Only the location changes, depending on what part of the country you hear it. (This tale, because of the ending, is a great favorite with children when I tell stories in schools.)

Tennessee ghost tales comprise just one small part of the great body of American folklore; but they play a very important part because of what these tales say about us as a people, of our beliefs, and even how we evolved as a society. Stories are passed down orally over the generations and are ever changing with the teller and the times. Traditional tales are sometimes thoroughly modernized to appeal to the present generation of listeners. Covered wagons and ox carts become horses and buggies, and horses and buggies become automobiles. But the basic stories remain the same.

When the motorcar first appeared on the rutted wagon trails of America, a whole new folklore appeared describing the efforts of motorists to keep their infernal contraptions in working order—the old story of man versus machine. The invention of the motorcar also influenced the evolution of the nature of folklore. This evolution is most easily seen in the so-called "bloody tales from lovers' lane."

"Bloody tales" are scary stories of homicidal maniacs and

assorted monsters that lurk in out-of-the-way places—namely lovers' lanes—and prey on unsuspecting couples. The tales are mainly of the slice-and-dice variety—bloody and often excessively gory. The object of the telling, of course, is for the boy to scare the girl out of her wits so she moves closer to him and gives him a convenient excuse to put his arm around her for "protection."

One of the more popular Tennessee tales in this genre involves a haunted tree, infested by the vengeful spirit of a murdered long hunter. When the monster happens upon a couple parked in a lonely lovers' lane, the horrible thing attacks. It reaches out with its terrible limbs, grabs its victim, drags him/her into a large hole in its trunk, and the person is seen no more. Outlandish to be sure, but a highly effective tale told on a dark night.

One person who told me the story was a Johnson City teenager who thought he had an exclusive and was clearly disappointed when he learned that I had heard the tale before. A few years before he died, my grandfather said that he had told the same story to my grandmother while they were courting, around the turn of the twentieth century. They were seated in a horse and buggy parked on a lonely wind-swept hill. He said that she was suitably frightened by the tale, moved closer to him on the buggy seat, and that was the beginning of a beautiful relationship that eventually yielded a dozen children.

These tales are not only wide-ranging and ageless, but are highly adaptive. The advent of the automobile, with its closed cab (for privacy, of course) and its ability to go a lot farther in a shorter amount of time than a horse and buggy, changed the methods of courting forever. As one appalled North Carolina man told a WPA worker in the late 1930s: "You talk about amusements, I think one of the worst things these days is the way young boys and girls do their courting. Most of them have automobiles, and instead of calling on the girls at home they drive out into the country. I've heard the girls talk about parking on a side road in the dark.... I am crazy about my girl, and I'd hate to think of her having to entertain her boyfriend in an automobile parked on the road-side."

Yes, indeed. Cars certainly did change the method of courting, but the courting itself remained essentially the same, and the bloody tale from lovers' lane survived the onslaught of technology.

In the past my readers have asked me about other ghost stories that I might have collected and why I did not include them in my books. My answer was that I wanted to stick to Southern ghost lore. But in *More Haunted Tennessee*, I thought I would try something a little different. The unofficial purpose of this tome is to demonstrate the sheer range of ghost lore that many suppose to be exclusive to Tennessee. So instead of presenting only Tennessee-based ghost lore, I offer some similar stories from other parts of the country to illustrate how widespread these motifs really are.

Some of the stories in this book are over two hundred years old. Some are brand new. The creatures of our imaginations are as vivid for us today as they were for our ancestors. So sit back and relax, and let your mind take you where it will. Whatever is out there lurking in the shadows will make its horrible self known—perhaps sooner than you think!

Charles Edwin Price
Winter 1999

The Screaming Phantoms of the Unakas

"Ghost logic" dictates that "true" ghosts will perform in pre-dictable ways. Their mystical behavior is repeated over and over again like a movie film played in an endless loop. (I know. I've used that analogy on and on, ad nauseam. But it's the best way I know how to describe the phenomenon.) The ghost of Abraham Lincoln, for example, is said to pace the corridors of the White House during periods of national emergency, his hands clasped behind his back and his head hung in profound thought. And, according to legend, the shade of Lincoln—in the White House, at least—has never been seen to do anything else.

Likewise, the screaming, headless ghost of Catherine Howard (a victim of her womanizing husband, Henry VIII) is said to race through the halls of Hampton Court in England with her head tucked underneath her arm. Poor Kate lost that part of her anatomy to the headman's axe. Unlike her stoic predecessor, Anne Boleyn, she went to her execution kicking and screaming all the way. Her ghost doesn't float down the staircase, nor does she appear at the foot of someone's bed in the middle of the night. She runs and screams. That's it.

It is also said that many ghosts, when they do appear, re-enact their last moments on Earth. Therefore, ghosts are some-times perceived as nothing more than fleeting shadows frozen in time. Ghosts are not considered to be thinking, reasoning entities. As such they pose no threat to the living—unless, of course, the living just happens to be utterly terrified at an unexpected sighting and suffers a coronary on the spot.

A little tale from Unicoi County illustrates this idea of "ghost logic" perfectly, especially the part about re-creating last moments. This blast from the past is also an ideal example of a trickster tale.

The Unaka Mountains, on the Tennessee/North Carolina border, contain some of the most rugged peaks in the Appalachian chain. Steep slopes, deep valleys, and shadowy hollows defeat travel except by railroad or modern highway. In fact, considering its almost perpendicular topography, it's a small wonder that the western slope of the mountains ever got settled at all. But two hundred years ago pioneers from the Carolina flatlands, with only crude wagons or a horse to carry their belongings, crossed the Unakas to make their homes in what would later become the state of Tennessee.

These white settlers were full of hope and anxious to make a new beginning in a virgin land. Most were displaced Scots-Irish who had been persecuted in North Carolina by a colonial governor, William Tryon, who considered them troublemakers. Many joined a revolutionary group called the Regulators. Tryon, himself, led the militia that defeated the upstarts at the Battle of Alamance in 1771. Ex-Regulators fled to the land west of the Alleghenies and out of the reach of Tryon and his associates.

The new immigrants entertained high hopes that their lives would improve in the west. For a while it looked as if that might be the case. Game was plentiful and the rivers were full of fish. The ground was fertile and there were plenty of building materials. Even the Cherokee Indians they encountered along the way seemed friendly. The natives permitted their new neighbors to build cabins and grow crops on their hunting grounds.

Unfortunately the Indians and the whites misunderstood each other from the very beginning. The Indians, it turned out, were only letting the whites borrow the land. It was not in the nature of the Cherokee, or any other Native American tribe in the area, to claim ownership of any parcel of real estate. They thought that the land belonged to everyone. The Cherokee claimed only territorial rights and felt that they were being more than benevolent in allowing the whites to borrow their hunting grounds.

The whites, on the other hand, didn't see it that way. They were under the impression that the Indians had *actually sold* them the land, and acted accordingly. Furthermore, when word drifted back to tidewater Carolina that the land out west was so rich that it would grow fantastic quantities of anything, and that there was so much game in the sumptuous forests that the animals practically fought their way into the traps, others, too, loaded their wagons and headed west.

As more people arrived to homestead, the Cherokee began to have second thoughts about their charity. They asked themselves, "Are our hunting grounds to be given over to these white farmers—our game killed to feed white families while ours starve?"

The annoyed Indians asked the whites to move on. The whites refused. They had put down their roots, they had built their cabins, they had planted their crops, and they intended to stay. So a violent and bloody war broke out on the frontier.

Isolated white families, with miles separating them from their neighbors, were forced to defend themselves against overwhelming odds. One family, their cabin located on the banks of Indian Creek in what is now eastern Unicoi County, Tennessee, was brutally massacred by Indian raiders. Every last one of them died a horrible death. Their horribly mutilated bodies were found weeks later by long hunters. Their cabin was burned to the ground and the crops were destroyed. No one ever caught the Indians who had done it.

Today the site of the slaughter is rich farmland, but the ghosts of the murdered are said to still walk the dark and bloody ground. Over the years stories of phantoms, seen and unseen, filled the enormous reservoir of Unicoi County folklore. Naturally such tales attracted the attention of adventurous boys.

One of these young lads was nicknamed Sandy. His buddy

was Albert—Al for short. Both of their families were farmers—hard nosed, practical, God-fearing parents who didn't believe in ghosts. Sandy and Al asked their parents for permission to go out to the old cabin site and watch for ghosts. The reply to both of them was a resounding "NO!" But they decided to go anyway. Al and Sandy knew they were taking a big chance, but the excitement they felt greatly outweighed the risk of discovery.

The moon was high, the autumn landscape bathed in silvery light. Indian Creek gurgled down the mountainside on its way to a rendezvous with the Nolichucky River four miles away.

Staring intently at the rough outcropping of limestone that marked the site of the former cabin, Al and Sandy waited patiently behind a clump of bushes. It was the anniversary of the massacre. Would they actually see ghosts? They didn't have to wait long to find out.

Sandy took a sharp breath as he saw a woman run noiselessly from the shelter of a stand of trees, apparently fleeing in terror. Close behind was a young boy of about twelve or thirteen. Behind him several Indians were in hot pursuit, tomahawks poised over their heads.

Al raised up over the bushes so he could see better. Terrified, Sandy tried to pull him down. Sandy wanted to run away but his legs wouldn't cooperate. Then both heard a twig snap. Al and Sandy wheeled around just in time to see two fierce painted Indians staring straight at them. Panicked, Al and Sandy forgot the ghosts. They yelped in terror, scrambled to their feet, and fled the thicket.

The two "Indians" watched the terrified boys disappear into the night. Then they grinned and slapped each other on the back, laughing and congratulating themselves.

Both fathers, all dressed up in makeshift Indian garb and wearing thick war paint, had taught their sons a valuable lesson that they would never forget. The men had known all along that their sons would try to sneak out that night to watch ghosts down by the old cabin, and they had been planning this caper all day. It had been more of a success than either had ever dreamed.

Sandy's father looked over toward the jumble of rocks and said, "That was certainly a fine touch you had, getting those people over there to put on buckskins and run around like that. It certainly added the proper atmosphere."

Al's father frowned and a funny look came over his face. "I didn't get them," he said uneasily. "I thought that you did."

Both men felt a sudden chill. They slowly turned toward the site of the old cabin as the ghostly images of long-ago murdered men, women, and children, as well as their attackers, slowly faded into the night. They had planned all day to play a joke on their sons. Now they realized that the joke had been on them!

NOTE: Another trickster tale with less than a happy ending, but similar, is the following as told to a WPA worker in the late 1930s by a German immigrant living on Long Island, New York. She had brought the tale over with her from Germany. Her phrasing and manner of speech are preserved in the following:

There was a nice farm close by us what was owned by a father and son, and they kept a working man there to work for them. His name was Heinrich. He was a very big, strong fellow and he worked hard, and he knows everything about a farm—horses and cows and pigs and chickens and everything.

So one time they all spreading manure on the ground and Heinrich says too warm the weather is, and he goin' to do his work at night time.

And the farmer says, "What's the matter mit you? Are you crazy you want to go to work in the night?"

And son of the farmer says to Heinrich, "Heinrich," he says, "the ghosts will come by you in the night time. Better you work by me in daylight, no?"

And Heinrich says he ain't scared of ghosts and even he ain't scared of the Devil yet, and he goin' to do more work in night time. So the farmer says to go ahead and the son of the farmer says to watch out the ghosts don't get you.

So the next night when the other people goin' to bed, about eight o'clock when it's getting dark, Heinrich gets manure wagon out and gets horses the stable out, and he gets the fork and commence to spread manure on the fields. And he makes good work and it's nice and cool and the moon shining down, and he's glad the boss lets him work in the night. And after, when the moon goes in, it gets more darker but Heinrich, he can see good yet. And he gets hungry after while and he says soon he goin' feed those horses, and then he's goin' by the kitchen and eat some bread and sausage after he's made empty the load what's on his wagon.

Well, Heinrich looks up and them two horses is shaking all over and he says, "What's the matter now?" he says. And quick he looks by some big trees by the woods where the corner of the field is and "Heiliger Gott!" he says, and he makes the sign of the cross. He can see a big white thing the trees between, and waving the arms up and down. And them horses is so scared they goin' to run away. He holds them by the head and he speaks to them. And he looks the trees between again and he didn't could see no ghost no more. So he goes to work yet and he makes empty the wagon and he takes his horses to the barn and gives them water and feed them, and then he goes by the kitchen and eats his bread and sausage. And after when the horses is through eating, he puts them back again in the wagon and he goes to work again till daylight comes, and the farmer and the son of the farmer comes out.

So the son of the farmer says, "Heinrich," he says, "did the ghosts been scaring you?"

And he says, "No," he says, "I didn't could be scared by such humbugs."

And the son of the farmer says, "What you could do when a ghost come and catch you yet?"

And he says, "I fix that ghost and when it is the Devil what comes by me, I fix him too."

And in the breakfast time the farmer and the wife and the son of the farmer makes foolishness by Heinrich, and the son says, "He's very brave fellow and the Devil couldn't make him scared."

Well, when night time come again Heinrich went with the horses out, same like before, and he spreads again the manure, maybe two or three loads. And just when the moon goes in he is close near the corner of the field where is the woods. And them horses start shaking again and Heinrich jumps quick out of that wagon to talk to them horses, and he has in his hand that manure fork. And quick he looks the trees between, and comes out now the ghost, same like last night, waving mit the arms. So first he makes the sign of the cross and then runs fast by that ghost and he hits him so hard he could on the head with heavy, iron manure fork, and that ghost falls down and don't make no noise.

Now, them horses so scared is they start to run away with wagon, and Heinrich he's running after them, but they don't stop no more till they come by the house. And Heinrich is holler out for horses to stop and make so much racket his boss and the wife comes quick out to see what loose is. And Heinrich says, "Kommen quick," he says. "I catched ein ghost."

And they all run fast by the corner where those trees is and they see white ghost on ground, mit horns sticking from his head out. And then they look very close and the wife of the farmer picks up those horns in the hand. And she picks up a bed sheet and down on the ground is the son of the farmer, and the son of the farmer is dead!

The One That Got the Fisherman

Ever since the prophet Jonah was swallowed by the great fish as punishment for trying to run away from God, stories have been told about people swallowed by oversized denizens of the deep. In folklore, every culture has such a story. Even the Cherokee Indians tell of a monster fish in the Nolichucky River that preyed on unfortunate warriors who crossed its path.

Every decent-sized body of water contains at least one elusive, scaly monster roaming its depths. I would suppose that everyone has heard of the Loch Ness Monster of Scotland. And in America there is the mysterious "Champ" who lurks in Lake Champlain, and the slippery "Chessie" who plies the depths of the Chesapeake Bay.

Large bodies of water, however, certainly do not have a corner on harboring gigantic fish. We hear of deep holes in rivers where the "granddaddy of all fish" is said to lurk. This immense specimen defeats every effort of fishermen to catch him, and he grows—as do stories about him—every year. Finally he becomes a great monster—no longer a mere fish, but a legend!

There is no doubt that giant fish exist in Tennessee. For instance, some catfish in Boone Lake have been known to reach six and seven feet in length. They are sluggish, unindustrious beasts that usually hang out by the floodgates at the dam, waiting for a handout. Divers cleaning the floodgates are obliged to push the pesky beasts out of the way so that they can get their work done.

Now, everyone has heard fish tales about the one that got away. The following is a fish tale, but it's not about the one that got away. It's about the one that got the fisherman.

"He's the granddaddy of them all," Grandpa told his grandson Woodrow. "He's the biggest fish anyone ever saw." Then the old man frowned as he added, "And he's a dangerous varmint to tangle with. No one I know will even try it."

Woody couldn't imagine any fish being so dangerous that it would scare a dyed-in-the-wool fisherman away, except maybe a shark. And he felt sure that no sharks lived in the Clinch River. But, at the same time, he wondered why such a large prize had not been pursued by other fishermen in the area. Certainly they all knew about Ol' Jake—that ancient fish who lurked in a deep hole in the river. But no one had tried to catch him. Why?

Of course, Woody had to find out.

"I'm warning you," Grandpa said, shaking a finger at his grandson. "If you know what's good for you, you'll stay away from that fish! I saw him once, swimming around down there in that deep hole where he lives. He's as big as a house!"

Old wives' tales, Woody sniffed. Grandpa was full of them.

It was inevitable, considering his eternal dedication to the almighty fishing pole—as well as his highly tuned sense of adventure—that Woody would try to catch Ol' Jake himself. He never thought for a moment that he wouldn't be successful. Then after he'd hauled him in, Woody would mount the head on the wall and charge the neighbors a nickel to see it. In no time at all he'd be rich!

Early the next morning, Woody hitched up the family horse to the wagon and set out for the Clinch River three miles away. He arrived a half hour later and tied the horse to a nearby tree. Then he unloaded his line and hook from the back of the wagon. He had also brought along a thick piece of salt pork to use as bait.

Woody didn't question for a moment that Ol' Jake was a

big fish. So his line was a piece of stout rope and his hook was made from a baling hook. He skewered the salt meat to the point of the hook and threw the whole thing into the river with a splash. Then he sat down to wait for a bite. It wasn't long in coming.

Something hit the bait with such force that it almost jerked Woody into the water. Woody pulled back sharply, hoping to snag whatever had struck. But the rope went limp in his hand and he was certain that nothing was on the other end.

He pulled in his line. He was right. The hook was bare. "Dang it!" Woody shouted out loud, "That stupid fish took my bait!"

Woody's horse, still tied to the tree, started to nicker and snort. Then he began to whinny loudly. Woody looked up. "What's the matter with you?" he growled.

Woody felt something hot and wet at the back of his neck. He turned around and saw a huge open mouth, with sharp teeth, staring him in the face. He tried to run away but it was too late.

With one gulp Ol' Jake swallowed Woody whole!

Woody slid down the fish's gullet and landed in his stomach with a splash. The liquid around him burned his skin—acid—digestive juices! Woody realized that he had to find a way out of the fish pronto or he would be eaten up alive!

The boy couldn't see a thing. It was pitch-black dark. It was also hot and stifling—not much air. When he stood up he was ankle deep in burning stomach juice and it was getting deeper by the second. Suddenly Woody had an idea. He reached into his pocket for the jackknife his grandfather had given him for his birthday. Luckily he had just sharpened it.

Woody made his way to the wall of the fish's stomach. He paused for a moment and wondered how Ol' Jake might react to being stabbed from the inside. Oh well, he thought, it couldn't be any worse than the pickle he was in now.

Woody took a deep breath, and with a mighty thrust he plunged his knife into the stomach of the fish. Almost immediately there came a shaking and shivering like an earthquake. Woody stabbed with the knife again, this time ripping a long bloody slash in the tough membrane.

More shaking. Woody could hardly keep his feet. With much effort he crawled out through the gash and fell into a slimy, evil-smelling mass. He stood up, trying to keep his footing on the slime. Then he made his way in the dark to what he believed was the side of Ol' Jake. Yes, this was it. He could feel the rib bones.

He plunged his knife into the flesh. Everything started shaking again. A deep roar was heard all about him. He plunged his knife into Ol' Jake again. Again and again Woody stabbed into the side of the monster. With every stroke of the knife there was more roaring and shaking. Suddenly the unsteady mass that he was standing on gave way and Woody found himself flat on his back.

Woody realized that the side of the fish was now above his head. Ol' Jake had flopped over on his side. Possibly he was dying. Woody stood up and continued his hacking. Warm, sticky liquid covered his face. He knew that it was Ol' Jake's blood. Now when he stabbed there was no reaction from the fish. A moment later he saw daylight through the little hole that he had managed to hack through the side of the fish. Fifteen minutes later he was outside and standing on Ol' Jake's side.

Woody dove into the water and swam for shore. Exhausted from his battle and his swim against the strong current of the river, he pulled himself onto the bank with a great effort. He lay on his stomach for a long time, breathing heavily.

He could hear thunder from an approaching storm overhead as he rolled onto his back. Woody raised up on one elbow and looked across the river. Ol' Jake floated on his side, one dead eye staring straight up, his body slowly drifting downriver. *He'll never eat anyone again*, Woody thought to himself.

Woody's arms and legs were stinging from the digestive juices in Ol' Jake's belly. He held his arm up to scratch it. The arm was chalk white. He held up his other arm. That was chalk white, too.

He stood up. His clothes were in tatters, but he could readily see that both legs were dead white. Panicked, Woody looked into a still pool at the side of the river. One glance told him that his face and head had suffered the same fate. The digestive juices inside the fish had taken all the color from his skin. He looked like a living ghost—his punishment for trying to catch Ol' Jake!

The big fish had its revenge. Woody looked like a living ghost for the rest of his life!

Race from the Graveyard

There used to be a widespread belief that graveyards—especially older graveyards, overgrown from lack of care, forgotten, and stuck out in the middle of nowhere—were haunted. Ghosts of the departed reside there waiting to pounce on the unwary passerby. Graveyards were to be avoided at all costs, especially after dark.

The folklore of the South teems with tales of haunted graveyards. There is, for instance, the well-known case of a small cemetery just off Main Avenue in Erwin. It it supposedly the home of the ghost of a monstrous hobo carrying a long, sharp knife. He waits for a victim to enter his territory in the dead of night. Then....

Of course there are the "Black Aggie" stories—apparitions of dead witches climbing out of their graves to haunt the living. Nearly any graveyard of size—in the city, town, or country—has at least one Black Aggie lurking among the tombstones. Maybe two.

Sometimes a Black Aggie is not a ghost at all. The most famous Black Aggie was supposed to haunt Druid Hill Cemetery in Baltimore, Maryland. After newspaper publisher Felix Angus died in the 1920s, his tombstone featured the statue of a small black angel resting on top of the monument. According to local legend, the angel's eyes would glow red at midnight and other ghosts in the graveyard would gather around the Black Aggie. It was also said that no grass would grow in the shadow of the statue and that a pregnant woman who wandered by would miscarry. The statue became something of a tourist attraction and caused quite a stir. Finally, to prevent desecration, the Angus family had the statue removed in 1967 and then gave it to the Smithsonian Institution. That august body, however, has not put it on display. We can only wonder why.

Do ghosts really haunt graveyards? There are some who say no. One day, as we were walking through the old town cemetery at Jonesborough, the late Bristol psychic Lena Jones told me that there is no such thing as ghosts in graveyards. "Only the dust is here," she said. "The spirits are somewhere else."

Lena may be right. But when imagination comes into play on a dark, moonless night, logic, like Black Aggie, flies out the window. Take, for example, this oft-told tale of a nightly encounter with a graveyard and ghost. It's a story I heard in Greene County.

A young man and his aged grandfather were once walking alone along a dark country road late at night. There was no moon to light the way, although an impotent light came from a splash of thousands of stars scattered overhead.

The old man was quite feeble and limped along with the aid of a cane. He had to be very careful lest his feet get tangled up in the ruts on the road and he fall. His grandson, on the other hand, had the agility of a spring deer.

Although they had begun their journey in the afternoon while the sun was still high, the old man's frequent need for rest had extended their trip much longer than planned. Grandfather was often out of breath and had to sit down by the wayside to regain his strength. His patient grandson, although anxious to reach their destination, would sit with him by the side of the road until the old man was ready to go again. The last thing in the world that he wanted to do was to leave the old man alone.

Along about midnight, the grandfather ran out of breath

again and plopped down on a convenient stone by the side of the road. His grandson joined him on a nearby rock.

The young man looked around and suddenly noticed there were many curious white stones near the side of the road— all about the same size and curiously shaped with rounded tops, almost as if fashioned by human hands. *Strange*, he thought to himself. *What oddly shaped rocks. I wonder how they got here?*

His question was soon answered when a glowing, translucent figure joined the pair and sat down on a rock beside them.

"There don't seem to be but three of us here tonight," the ghost commented blandly.

One quick look and the young fellow leaped to his feet. He suddenly realized that a cemetery skirted the road at that point. The grandfather, who had also seen the ghost, was trying to struggle to his feet.

"Yeah, but there ain't gonna be but the two of you in a minute," the boy shouted back at the apparition. He took off like a shot, disregarding his grandfather's appeals not to be left behind.

As the grandson ran down the road, he surprised a rabbit hurrying along. The animal was in his way and was certainly not running fast enough for the boy. "Git outta there, rabbit," the grandson shouted as he passed the scurrying animal like it was standing still. "Let somebody run that can run."

It was five long miles to home, but the terrified youth made it in record time. Just as he reached home and tried to close the door after him, he felt someone pushing against it. The terrible thought crossed his mind that it might be the ghost behind him.

Then he heard his grandfather's feeble voice say, "Don't slam the door in your poor old grandpappy's face, son."

NOTE: *A police officer, working in Johnson City, told me the following little story about his grandfather's experience with a rural graveyard in the Tiger Creek area of Carter County:*

Grandfather, when he was courting, used to ride horseback. He had been to see my grandmother. They had been to church—in fact they had met each other for the first time at church.

He was on his way home after dark on horseback. He was riding past a cemetery on a hill. As he came through this little stretch of road, he saw what appeared to be a very attractive young lady run across the road in front of him and the horse. The young lady was completely nude. She made no sounds— didn't say anything—as she ran off into a laurel thicket to the side of the road.

At the sight, his horse reared up and tried to throw him off. He got the horse under control, dismounted, and yelled into the direction where she had disappeared, but he got no reply.

Since it was dark he did not attempt to go off into the laurel thicket after her. And he never knew for certain if it was a real lady or something else, but he was sure about what he saw.

Ghost in the Closet

Sometimes it seems ghosts can bear a grudge. And when they return to this world for vengeance, watch out!

Western Maryland has its tale of "Wailing Willie," the ghost of a railroad brakeman who was killed as the result of a practical joke by his fellow workers. For years passenger trains on the Western Maryland Railroad were supposed to be haunted by the leering specter of Willie, who would run through the cars, wailing at the top of his voice, terrorizing passengers.

In Edinburgh, Scotland, there is the story of Angus Roy, a sailor who suffered a tragic accident on a ship and was forced to leave his trade. Because of his accident, not only was he a cripple, but he was also cursed with a hideously disfigured face. Kids taunted him for the rest of his life. Angus always swore that he would come back when he died and haunt the little urchins. Apparently he does. In the dead of night children in Edinburgh are often visited by old Angus at their bedsides. His wispy figure appears at the foot of their bed moaning loudly, his hands reaching out for them. Of course, the kids are scared to death and spend the rest of the night with their parents.

Our next tale is remarkably similar to the Scottish tale of old Angus. It takes place, however, in Johnson City. Johnson City is progressive, ever moving forward. But, here, too, the unknown dwells—hiding in the shadows—waiting for the right moment to pounce on the unsuspecting.

Twelve-year-old Janet was afraid to go to bed at night. She just knew there was something in her bedroom closet waiting to snatch her up and take her to some dreadful place. She was absolutely sure of it. Such a thing had happened before, and there was a good chance that it would happen to her. A terrifying incident that occurred just the week before only confirmed her worst fears.

At about two in the morning Janet was sound asleep. Suddenly a loud noise woke her up. She sat up in bed just in time to see her closet door slowly creak open. Two eyes appeared, glowing in the darkness.... Then a shape.... Then something that looked like a distorted head. Then a clutching, bony hand stretched out for her from the darkness.

Janet screamed. Her mother came running. "What's wrong?" her mother shouted.

"It's coming after me," Janet cried in a panic. "It's in the closet."

"What's in the closet?"

"The awful thing that got little Johnny Patterson. It got him and now it's trying to get me."

Janet's mother shook her head. She tried to tell Janet that there was nothing in the closet but clothes and discarded toys. She even went inside and searched all around, nearly tripping over a box full of old dolls in the process.

When she returned she said, "See? There's nothing in there. It didn't get me."

Janet shook her head. "It's not you that it wants," she sobbed. "It's me!"

"I wonder what's wrong with that girl?" Janet's father grumbled the next morning as his wife served him breakfast. "She's twelve years old. You'd think she'd be over the bogeyman under the bed by now."

Janet looked up from her cereal and frowned. "It's not under the bed, Daddy. It's in the closet!"

"Whatever," her father sighed in frustration. "I made a big mistake telling you the history of this house in the first place.

I never thought you'd take that wild tale so seriously."

But Janet *had* taken the story seriously. Her father would have taken it a lot more seriously too, that is if he had seen the thing in her closet—that slimy, gross, drooling, red thing.

Just after they had moved into the house, Janet's father told her of the events that occurred not only long ago, but also a short time before. The house had been built about fifty years ago by an elderly man who hated kids. The feeling was mutual. The neighborhood kids hated him because he was so mean to them. The children made the situation much worse by constantly teasing the old man and playing tricks.

After one of their pranks—like the time someone dumped a whole carton of sour milk on his front stoop—the old man would tear up and down the neighborhood ranting and raving, swearing that he would get even with the little brats if it was the last thing that he ever did. That energetic response, of course, just made some of the more unruly kids more determined to aggravate him even more. So they continued to play pranks. One time, however, things went too far.

It was about ten o'clock on a really dark night. The old man was preparing to go to bed. One of the neighborhood boys had a new rubber fright mask that he had bought at a local novelty shop. He thought it would be funny to put on the mask and stare in the window at the old man—just like a monster would do.

The boy with the mask, and two of his friends, climbed up on the roof of the front porch of the old man's white-frame house. The boys could easily stand on the roof of the porch and peer through the window into the room. When the boys peeped in the window, the light was on in the bedroom but no one was there.

"Where is he?" one of the boys whispered to the others.

"Don't know," came the reply.

Suddenly the faint sound of a flushing toilet was heard. Then the old man hobbled through the bedroom door.

The boys ducked. One of them put on the rubber mask. "This'll get him," he snickered. Then he raised back up and peered through the window.

The old man was now in his closet rummaging through a pile of clothes, obviously looking for something. Suddenly he got the feeling that someone was watching him. He wheeled around and caught sight of the horrible face staring at him through the window. The old man threw up his hands and screamed. Then he clutched his chest.

The boys panicked. Something was dreadfully wrong with the old man. His eyes bugged out like a frog's and his face turned cherry-red. The boys did not wait to see what would happen next. They turned, ran across the porch roof, clambered down the posts, jumped to the ground, and ran off into the night.

The old man was not seen for several days after that, and his neighbors began to worry about him. Sure he was an old fussbudget, but he was also a human being. The neighbors didn't know about the prank that the boys had played. And, of course, the boys were not talking.

Curious neighbors soon discovered the body of the old man in the closet, dead from an apparent heart attack. The coroner chalked up the heart attack to age and that was the end of that.

Or was it?

A family named Patterson had owned the house before Janet's family. They had one child, a ten-year-old boy named Johnny.

Johnny had the same bedroom as Janet had now. And it was the same bedroom that the old man had occupied the night that he died.

One night, Johnny's mother heard him scream. She ran into the bedroom just in time to see a horrible, hook-like hand thrust from behind the open door of the closet, grab her son, and drag him inside.

She ran into the closet but found nothing. Panicked, she called her husband. Together they literally tore that closet apart, even to the point of partially tearing out the back wall. Of course all they found was wood and plaster—but no Johnny.

Three days later Johnny mysteriously reappeared, apparently none the worse for wear. But he couldn't remember where he had been, nor could he remember anything about the three days he had been missing. What had happened to him?

As soon as the neighbors heard about young Johnny, they offered their own explanations to his parents.

"Your boy's room is the same one that the old man slept in," one said, "and your son's closet was that same closet in which he died! I've heard he haunts that closet and that any kid who uses the bedroom is sure to get kidnapped by the ghost."

Another neighbor agreed. "That old man swore vengeance on all children because they tormented him so much. Those kids tortured that old man right into a heart attack. We found out about it later. That's what happened to Johnny. I'll bet you that the old man's ghost kidnapped him for revenge."

Although they failed to totally swallow the story about the vengeful old man's ghost in the closet, things were getting a bit too creepy for the Pattersons. They certainly would never use that infamous room again. In fact, little Johnny would not even go near it. His mother figured that he remembered more than he was letting on. Otherwise, why would he be so scared?

There was nothing else they could do. The Pattersons put the house up for sale.

Janet's father thought he was getting a real bargain when he was quoted a price for the house. The real estate agent said that the owners were having financial difficulties and had to sell in a hurry. Of course, she was only telling a half-truth. The Pattersons were spending a fortune on a psychiatrist to help Johnny, but they were not in financial difficulty—at least not yet. They just wanted to unload the property and were willing to accept any reasonable offer.

After the deal was closed, Janet's father learned that the house had a reputation for being haunted by the ghost of a vengeful old man who hated kids. But he didn't believe in ghosts, and neither did Janet—at least she didn't until that terrifying encounter with the face in the closet.

"You were having a nightmare," her father told her the morning after her ghastly encounter. "That's all."

"Can I sleep in another room?" Janet pleaded.

"No, you cannot!" her father replied emphatically. "It's time you started to grow up and stop believing in old wives' tales!"

A week after she first saw the ghost in the closet, Janet was getting ready for bed. The passage of time had somewhat dulled her fear of being alone in the room, but she was still skittish about turning off the light. Her mother tucked her under the covers and reached for the lamp.

"No," Janet said. "Don't do that!"

Janet's mother sat down on the bed beside her and took her daughter's hand. "There's nothing in that closet," she said patiently. "I checked while you were taking your bath. And I checked again while you were drying your hair."

"B-but...."

"No buts about it," her mother said sternly. "Your father said that you were going to have to get over this fear, and I agree."

Janet smiled weakly and nodded. With a click the lights went out in the room.

Then her mother went to bed.

An hour later a terrible pounding shook the house. Janet thought it was an earthquake. Then there was silence. Janet sat up slowly in the bed. Sweat formed in little beads on her forehead.

Suddenly the closet door started to creak open.

Janet's eyes grew wide with terror. Something horrible was inside that closet and it was coming after her. She tried to scream, but her throat was so dry that she couldn't make a sound. Her heart beat like a bass drum.

Where were her parents? Surely they must have heard the terrible pounding. Why didn't they come?

Then from deep inside the closet she heard a noise that sounded like an angry cat. At the same moment two faint dots appeared, growing brighter by the moment. Eyes...those same horrible eyes that she had seen before...yellow...glowing.

Then the head arose...red like blood. The mouth was open, bowed in a horrible grin. Saliva dripped from the rims.

A bony hand reached out for her. It came closer. Then Janet felt it close around her arm in a terrible grip. She felt herself being pulled out of the bed. Then everything went dark.

Three days later, twelve-year-old Janet reappeared mysteriously—almost out of thin air. And, like Johnny, she said she couldn't remember a thing—where she had been or what had happened to her. Her frantic parents didn't waste one moment. They vacated the house and put it up for sale—at even more of a bargain than they had bought it. But they were quite sure, given its terrible reputation, the house would never sell again.

But they were wrong. There was always someone who would buy a nice house at a bargain price. So the evil spirit waited in the closet alone, a part of the walls, the plaster—the very beams and joists that kept the house from coming apart.

It would have its chance again, of that it was sure. Once again the house—its house—was up for sale. All it would have to do was wait.

And any family who bought it, especially if they had kids, would get more—much more—than they had bargained for.

Footprints in the Snow

Sometime in the nineteenth century mysterious cloven hoof-prints were found one morning in the snow in Devon, England. Their sudden appearance had the entire countryside seized in a grip of fear. Was it a devil—or worse—that had made the tracks? Needless to say, imaginations kicked into overdrive among the superstitious townsfolk, and the so-called "Devil of Devon" found a secure place in local folklore.

A somewhat similar tale of "devil's" footprints exists in Washington County, Tennessee, along the Nolichucky River. Here, too, mysterious cloven prints appear—so frequently, in fact, that the particular stretch of riverbank is known as "Devil's Run." All attempts to capture the creature who made the prints have come to naught.

A tale from Unicoi County tells of a very tiny devil that crawls out of Indian Creek and confronts small boys who have wandered away from home. The creature usually renders the child temporarily mute.

The devil is a popular figure in folklore. Being the personification of evil, he and his minions dwell on the earth in an attempt to lure humanity into the depths of sin. Apparently it is also Ol' Scratch's mission to terrorize the superstitious. One of these ways, obviously, is to lay down sets of mysterious footprints that cause our imaginations to go reeling.

The following story from Cumberland County is a tale about one of these sets of prints—this time, however, with a bizarre twist. I would not be surprised if this tale was directly related to the Devon or Nolichucky story. Folktales have a tendency to multiply like an atomic chain reaction and spread like a red hot rumor.

One very cold winter morning mysterious footprints appeared in freshly fallen snow on a hardscrabble farm in the Crab Orchard Mountains. The footprints were cloven and were only about an inch long. The distance between each print was about three inches, and whatever had made them had traveled in a perfectly straight line.

It was as if a tiny two-legged goat had taken a notion to make a trip across the countryside, not bothering to go around any obstacle—a tree or boulder—but had walked straight through them as if they weren't even there!

The prints were discovered by a young man who was out hunting rabbits. About two inches of dry snow had fallen overnight—a good time to spot rabbit tracks.

When the young fellow came upon the strange tracks, he couldn't make heads or tails of them. So he went home and asked his father to come see what he thought. The father, of course, had no idea what had made them either. So he called a friend and, together, the three of them tried to figure out what kind of creature had made the tracks.

"Let's follow them and see where they go," the friend suggested.

The trio followed the absolutely straight trail for several miles. Nothing blocked the path of the tracks. If a boulder was encountered, the tracks would end on one side of the boulder, then continue on the other side. There was no indication that the thing had climbed over the obstacle, because the snow on top was undisturbed. It was as if the creature had gone straight through the rock. The same thing happened when the tracks encountered a tree or other large solid object—the tracks would stop on one side and continue on the other.

"I've never seen anything like it!" the father said, scratching his head.

"I don't mind telling you," his friend remarked, "I'm getting a pretty creepy feeling about all of this. I don't think we should follow these tracks any farther. No telling what we might find on the other end."

But the father's curiosity was getting the best of him. He just had to discover what kind of creature had made them.

"At least send your boy back home," the friend suggested.

"No, Daddy," the boy pleaded. "I want to see, too."

The father admired the spirit of adventure in the boy. Besides, the man could protect his offspring if necessary. "Come on, boy," the father said, "but stick by me."

The trio followed the strange tracks for several more miles. All the time, they argued about who, or what, had made them. Certainly it was not an animal—at least a known animal. These tracks were obviously made by something that traveled on two legs. But if that were true, the creature must have been very small—less than a foot high.

"I'm getting scared," the boy told his father.

The father was getting a bit nervous himself. But he was also very curious. He wanted to continue.

"Over here!" the friend shouted. "Look at this!"

Father and son ran to where the man was standing, on the brink of a high cliff. The man pointed to the ground. The tracks reached the edge of the cliff, then disappeared over the edge. Cautiously, the father peered over the lip of the cliff.

"It must be two hundred feet straight down," he said. "Whatever it was must have fallen over and been killed."

But the boy was not so sure. As the trio turned toward home he could have sworn that he saw an impossibly small creature—it looked like an elf—running across the meadow at the base of the cliff. It turned toward him and grinned. The boy tried to tell his father to look but suddenly found he could not speak. And he did not regain his voice until he had returned home again. By that time, of course, there was no chance of catching up with the creature—whatever it was—to prove that he had really seen something.

Booger Tracks in the Cellar

This story is about an encounter with a booger—a word that many mountain people in the South still use to describe a mysterious ghost or spirit.

The way that I understand it, the word booger *comes from a literal translation of a Native American word for ghost or evil spirit. During meetings in council houses, medicine men stood outside the building wearing masks made from the bark of trees or even tanned animal faces. These were called* booger masks *and were supposed to frighten away any evil spirits in the vicinity.*

The word caught on with the whites, and even today the word is used to describe denizens of the supernatural. Usually wispy boogers leave no sign of their passing—but the booger in our story did.

"I knew it!" came the excited shout from the cellar. "I just knew it!"

Buford's grandfather clomped up the wooden basement steps like a sailor storming up a gangway. Breathing heavily he huffed into the living room and plopped into a ratty, overstuffed, brown chair resting near the fireplace.

"Now I'm sure this house is hainted," he said breathlessly. "I just found booger tracks in the cellar."

Buford looked up from the puzzle that he was working. He had frequently heard his grandfather declare that the white frame house on Unaka Avenue in Johnson City was haunted.

There were a bunch of strange noises in the house all right—lots of them. Everyone in the family—including Buford's skeptical father—had heard them at one time or another. Every night, the house played a nocturnal concert—pops, cracks, booms, and an occasional rustle. The scariest noise of all occurred just over Buford's bedroom. It sounded like someone was walking across the attic floor in cement sneakers.

Buford's daddy—practical as usual—had a ready explanation for the sounds. Old houses always made unexplained noises—especially in cold, wet weather. This house, he said, was over eighty years old and obviously suffered from structural lumbago.

"If you were as old as this house," he informed Buford, "your bones would pop, too."

That explanation did little to comfort the frightened boy. Every night, Buford lay in his bed, helpless as a suckling pig on the platter, and listened to the thumping overhead, knowing that no one would ever take them (or him) seriously. When he tried to crawl into his parents' bed for protection, his father chided the boy for being a spineless wimp.

"Noises can't hurt you!" his daddy grumbled.

"Leave the child alone, Harold," his mother said as she gathered the quivering bundle into her arms. "He's only a little boy."

"That little boy is twelve years old!" Harold Packwood shot back angrily. "He's old enough to sleep in his own bed and leave us to ours!"

Lately the noises in the house had subsided a tad. In fact, several peaceful months had passed since Buford had last padded into his parents' room at two in the morning, seeking the protection of their bed. Then just when everything was starting to look up and it seemed like the ghost had gone for good, Papaw had to up and find booger tracks in the cellar!

"What do booger tracks look like, Papaw?" Buford asked.

"Like brush marks on the dirt floor," his grandfather

answered. "Like someone has scraped a garden rake lightly over the dirt. We had booger tracks down at the old home place, too. We had plenty of boogers down there."

"How many?"

"At least a dozen, I reckon. One of them kept slamming your daddy's bedroom door at two o'clock in the morning. The racket woke up the whole house."

"Did Daddy get scared?"

"You're darn right he got scared! And don't let him tell you no different. Your daddy ran into our room in the middle of the night, just like you run into his, and tried to crawl into our bed, too."

Buford felt somewhat relieved that he was not the only wimp in the family. His father the lawyer, who was standing in the arched doorway between the living room and dining room, had overheard the conversation between his father and his son.

"No wonder the boy is like he is, Daddy!" Harold Packwood, Esq., growled as he strode angrily into the room. "Your grandson is already a bundle of nerves. You're just making things worse by filling his head with this booger tommyrot."

"Daddy," Buford said anxiously, "Papaw said he just saw booger tracks in the basement."

"No he didn't!" Harold shot back emphatically. "There are no such things as boo...GHOSTS! Circumstantial evidence doesn't support such a charge."

"And how do you know that?" Papaw calmly asked his son. "You certainly thought there was 'circumstantial evidence' when you were Buford's age. And," he added as an afterthought, "will you stop that silly lawyer talk about evidence? This ain't no courtroom."

Harold replied, "And I wish you'd stop using cutesy words like 'booger' and 'haint' to describe things you don't understand. You sound like you just came out of the hills."

"That's because I *did* come out of the hills," Papaw answered angrily. "And unless my memory fails me, so did you!"

You bet your boots Papaw came out of the hills. He had

been a dirt farmer all his life. The old home place, a five-room white clapboard house, was located on a fifty-acre farm near the Limestone community in Washington County. Recently Papaw had been forced to sell his house and land. The tiny pension he received from the government, coupled with the meager proceeds from his truck farm, did not cover his ever-growing expenses.

At sixty-two he was beginning to feel his age, and the fire burning in his belly had gotten worse over the past months. Sometimes the pain was so bad that he'd double over and it would be hard for him to breathe. His legs would buckle and he would drop to his knees. Thirty seconds later he would be all right again. He'd get up, catch his breath, and continue whatever he was doing before the attack.

Since Papaw hated doctors, he had avoided seeing one about the mysterious spells. Papaw's attacks frightened Buford, but even he could not convince his grandfather to see a doctor.

After his father had left the room, and Papaw had simmered down bit, Buford asked, "Do all ghosts leave booger tracks, Papaw?"

Papaw smiled. "No, boy. Booger tracks are special. They're magic. Boogers leave their tracks because they want you to see them and to let you know that they're around. They're trying to tell you something. But not everyone can see booger tracks—only folks with unclouded eyes. You've got to clear your mind of all grown-up things and concentrate on the booger tracks. Only then will they become visible."

"Is that why Daddy can't see them?" the boy asked.

Papaw glanced in the direction of the room where Buford's father had disappeared, and frowned. "My son is too busy being a red-hot lawyer to see the world as it really is," he growled. Then Papaw turned to his grandson. "When your daddy was little, he saw booger tracks all right. Lots of 'em. Now he can't see anything past the court docket."

"Can you still see them, Papaw? And can I see them, too?"

"I reckon so." Papaw turned toward the basement door. "Seeing booger tracks should come as natural to you as playing baseball. But, you know, there's only one way to find out for sure. Come on with me. Let's both go down into the cellar. We'll find out if you can really see the booger tracks."

The cellar was not the least bit spooky, usually. Buford had been down there a hundred times before, sometimes to play, sometimes to fetch tools for his father, sometimes just to hang out. But never in his wildest dreams did he ever imagine there might be a ghost lurking down there. If he had known that, he would have stayed away.

Buford and Papaw descended the rickety wooden steps and stepped onto the well-packed dirt floor. Buford looked around nervously. "Where are they, Papaw?"

Papaw pointed to a dark corner near the water heater. "Over there."

Buford moved to the white enamel water heater. His sharp eyes looked for any unusual markings on the floor. Suddenly he noticed what appeared to be fresh swish marks in the dirt—like someone in a long robe trailing the ground had passed by. "There," Buford declared.

"Yep! That's them, all right," his grandfather said.

"What kind of booger is it?" Buford asked.

"A ghost, I reckon," Papaw answered. "Ain't no troll or anything like that."

Buford's eyes widened. "But I thought ghosts didn't leave tracks—that they were all filmy and not solid or anything."

"Now that's where you're wrong, boy," Papaw declared. "Some ghosts are that way, sure—no substance to 'em. But others ain't. My father—your great-grandfather—once come upon a booger that looked just like a real man. He was solid and even left footprints in the snow. Now that don't sound like no wisp of smoke, does it?"

"No, sir. What happened?"

Papaw entered his story-telling mode, as he had done for Buford a thousand times before. "Well, now...," he began as he sat down on an empty wooden crate and Buford sat on the floor in front of him. "It had just come a snow. My folks were just married and, of course, there were no kids yet. The five of us came along much later.

"One day Daddy was outside chopping wood for Mama's stove. It was a cold evening in December, just before Christmas. It was still snowing and a couple of inches were already on the ground. Daddy had gotten winded and leaned against a tree to rest, when he saw a man standing way off in a grove of trees. The feller was just standin' there, watchin' him.

"Now in those days, folks walkin' on your land wasn't much cause for alarm. Sure there were hoboes and desperadoes, but they were few and far between. But my daddy said the way this feller was starin' made him mighty uneasy—it was as if he was lookin' straight through him.

"Suddenly, without warnin', the man disappeared. Daddy said he vanished into thin air. Daddy put down his axe and walked over to where the man had been standin' and saw fresh tracks in the snow—just one set of tracks. There was no tracks leading to, or away, from them, neither.

"Daddy knew for sure that he had seen a booger and that his woods was probably hainted. He told my mother about what he had seen, and she got so flustered that she never went into the woods again.

"When I was a little boy, Mama always warned me to stay out of those woods, too. Of course, I never listened."

"Did you ever see the ghost your daddy saw?" the wide-eyed Buford asked.

"Nope," his grandfather replied. "Never did. And nobody else ever did, neither. But that fact didn't calm my mother down none. Until the day she died she claimed the woods out behind the old home place was hainted, and she refused to set foot in them."

"But," Buford insisted, "did you believe the woods were haunted, Papaw?"

"Can't rightly say, Buford. Some tell that a rich man was killed by Indians in those woods—way back in the pioneer days. But that was just rumor. I don't know if there was any truth in it or not."

Buford took in a deep breath and let it out slowly. Then he looked down to the dirt floor of the cellar where the fresh scratch marks—booger tracks—were etched in the hard-packed dirt. He felt cold, although it was a warm summer day. It was always cooler in the cellar than the rest of the house, but now it was getting downright chilly. Suddenly Buford heard his grandfather gasp. *Oh, no*, he thought to himself. *Not another attack.* He turned and saw his grandfather staring at the cellar wall—at an area near the water heater.

Buford nearly jumped out of his skin. A ghastly white glow was materializing and, in its center, the shadowy outline of a face. In a few seconds the face was clear. It was that of an old man wearing a long white beard. Buford had seen the face before.

The face in the light was frightening but not unkindly. It looked with otherworldly eyes at the two standing there. The corners of its mouth were turned up in a faint smile. Then it opened its mouth and spoke in kind of a loud whisper.

"I see you found my message," the ghost said to Papaw.

"Daddy!" Papaw said in a voice barely above a whisper himself.

"It has been a long time, boy," the apparition replied. Then it turned and looked at Buford. "So, this is my great-grandson."

Buford backed away a few steps.

"Don't be frightened," the ghost said. "I won't hurt you. I just have some business with your grandfather, then I'll be on my way."

"What do you want with me, Daddy?" Papaw asked shakily.

"The farm," the ghost said sternly. "You flea-flappin' kid, you done went and sold the farm."

"I had to," Papaw replied. "I had no money."

"On the contrary, boy," the apparition replied. "You have plenty of money."

"What in the blazes are you talking about, Daddy?"

"Watch your language, son," the ghost admonished.

"Sorry," Papaw replied.

The apparition continued, "When you told Buford the story of me seeing that ghost—back before you were born—you didn't finish." The apparition turned to Buford. "I really did see a ghost in those woods years ago," it began, its voice growing stronger. "After the ghost disappeared, I searched the woods for a half hour and, then, I saw it again. It stood by an old, dead tree stump, pointing at the ground. Then the ghost spoke to me and said that it was the spirit of one of the first settlers in Limestone—a Scot who had brought a great deal of money with him to America. He buried it there by a tree but had been killed by Indians before he had a chance to use it. Now the ghost was telling me where it was."

"But we were always poor dirt farmers," Papaw protested. "If what the ghost said was true, why didn't you dig up the treasure yourself so we could have had a better life than we had?"

The ghost smiled. "Money doesn't make for a better life, son. Remember me telling you that when you were a boy? Was I right? Did you ever starve to death from what I made on that farm you sold from under me?"

"No, sir," Papaw answered, lowering his head.

"Besides," the ghost continued. "I was told by the ghost that somebody other than myself would have greater need of the money one day. Now I know what it meant. There's enough gold buried in that spot for you to buy back our farm and to keep you going for the rest of your life. The tree is now rotted away, but we both know someone who can show you exactly where the treasure is buried."

Buford could hardly believe his ears at what the ghost said next: "Save half the money you find for Buford. Keep it for his education—then give him the rest when he graduates from college."

Papaw frowned. "I don't think I'll live that long."

The ghost's hard expression softened. "Yes, you will, son," it said. "Doctors can fix what is wrong with you if you go see one. Don't be afraid. Use some of the money for that, too. I have it on the best authority that you have many years left to tell your outlandish tales to your grandson if you do what I say."

Papaw smiled. "Yes, sir."

"Promise me and your mother that you will see the doctor," the apparition insisted, its expression hardening again.

"I promise."

The ghost appeared to relax. "Good," it said. Then it vanished.

"Wait a minute, Daddy," Papaw shouted.

But no one was in the cellar except Buford and his grandfather. After a moment a very discouraged Buford said, "Now we'll never find the gold."

"Yes we will," Papaw said. "Remember what Daddy just said. We'll ask someone who knows."

"But who can we ask?" Buford asked. "The ghost is gone."

"You might be surprised," Papaw said as he turned toward the stairs and began climbing toward the first floor of the house. When they entered the living room, Buford's father was busily rummaging through some old papers in the upright secretary that stood in the corner. He looked up as Buford and his Papaw approached.

"I thought you might be coming, Daddy," Harold Packwood said. "I heard you talking in the cellar with your father."

Buford plopped down on a chair, an expression of utter confusion on his face. "I don't get it."

"You will," his father said.

Finally Harold found what he was looking for. It was a yellowed sheet of lined notebook paper with a map scrawled on it in faded pencil. He turned to Buford and held out the paper. "I believe this will answer most of your questions," he said.

Buford took the paper and examined it. He looked up at his father, a quizzical expression on his face.

Harold smiled. "Your great-grandfather visited my room many years ago, when I was a boy no older than you are now. He told me about the treasure and told me to draw this map." Then he turned to his father. "He also said not to show the map to your grandfather because he was a cantankerous cuss that would not believe that the sky was blue unless someone led him outside and showed it to him. Then my grandfather's ghost said not to dig up the treasure, but to keep the map in a safe place. He said I would know when it was the right time to retrieve it."

"B-but you said you didn't believe in ghosts."

Papaw took up the story. "Once, your daddy told me about the visit from his grandfather's ghost and the map just after the whole thing happened. But I told him that he should grow up and stop talking nonsense."

"So," Harold explained, "I put the map away. It's been hidden all these years—until now. I was afraid to mention the ghost or the map."

"When the ghost said that we both knew someone who might know where the treasure was buried," Papaw continued, "I suddenly remembered what your daddy had told me thirty years ago and I knew that he would be able to help."

Buford turned to his father. "You knew about boogers all along," he said. "And Papaw..."

"...is a great big storyteller," Papaw confessed. "You see, Buford, your daddy knew about the boogers. But since I created so much fuss when he tried to tell me about one of them, and the map...I couldn't really see booger tracks. I was just playing along with you. But you and your daddy.... Well, the truth was that your daddy believed in boogers all along just like you. I was the one who didn't believe in them!"

Road Kill

Can you always believe your eyes? Sometimes, you can't. Here's a tale from Kingsport about one fellow who couldn't believe his eyes, and he learned a valuable lesson in the process.

Sherman Steele loved to drive fast, and he considered the roads of Kingsport and Sullivan County his own private race track. Never mind the other drivers or pedestrians he might encounter along the way. Sherman thought that he was the only one who counted. Certainly he had been ticketed for speeding and reckless driving before, but had yet to have an accident—and isn't that what's important? He had never killed or injured a soul with his sports car. So the fun continued unabated.

Whenever Sherman got into his car he'd start her up, rev up the engine, and squeal out onto the open road. The car gave him a feeling of power—a sense of power that he felt nowhere else in his life.

Spring was here. It was warm. Today was the first day that Sherman had been able to put down the top on his car, and he was totally enjoying the weather. The wind whipped through his hair as he sped down the road—not a care in the world.

There was too much traffic for him on the old Highway 23, so he decided to get off that road. Sherman was coming up on the Fort Patrick Henry Dam on the Holston River and he knew of a side road he could take, just before he reached the dam.

The new road was narrow and twisting—the ideal place to drive a flashy sports car. Shortly after the turnoff, Sherman knew that he would approach an arched underpass that tunneled beneath a set of CSX Railroad tracks. The width of the arch was too narrow for two cars to pass each other. A sensible driver would have slowed down just in case another car was coming in the opposite direction. But not Sherman. A second car would just have to take its chances.

As Sherman approached the underpass, he saw a slight movement at the corner of the arch. Then an elderly woman in old-fashioned clothes, carrying two shopping bags, suddenly appeared, walking in the middle of the road. Sherman jammed on his brakes, but it was too late! His sports car barely missed a concrete abutment as it skidded across the roadway, hit the loose gravels on the side of the road, and ground to a stop in a cloud of dust. Sherman had missed the concrete arch, but he had hit the old lady—he just knew that he had. There was no way that he could have missed her.

For a long time Sherman rested his forehead on the steering wheel, staring at the floorboards of the car. He didn't dare to look back for fear of the sight of the bloody body he knew was lying in the middle of the road, groceries scattered all around. A minute later, when he finally did get the courage to look back, he was astonished to see no sign of the woman.

Sherman jumped from his car and ran up and down the road. Maybe she had been thrown into the bushes by the impact.

Nope! Nothing. There was no sign that she had even been there at all. No groceries. No blood. No nothing.

Could Sherman have been seeing things? Could the old woman have been a figment of his imagination?

Maybe he should report the accident to the police, even though there was no body.

No, he thought to himself. If he said anything to the cops

they would have to question him and then he'd have to admit he was speeding.

He might even lose his license.

No. He would keep quiet about the whole thing.

But Sherman was unable to sleep that night. The horrified expression of the old woman, just before he hit her, haunted him. Finally he couldn't stand it anymore. The next day he told a friend about his experience.

"Oh," his friend said knowingly. "You've met Annie?"

Sherman didn't know what his friend was talking about. An explanation was in order.

"About fifty or sixty years ago, an old woman was run down by a speeding motorist at that very archway," his friend explained to him. "The driver didn't see her and, well, she was hit flat out and was killed. For months afterwards, they found bits and pieces of her groceries in the woods beside the road—she was hit that hard. I'm surprised you didn't know about it."

Sherman shook his head.

"The story goes that every once in a while, when a driver is speeding on that stretch of road, the ghost of Annie will step out from behind that arch and get hit all over again—just to deliver a message."

"Don't tell me," Sherman interrupted. "I think I already know what the message is. Slow down. Right?"

"Right," his friend answered. Then he looked at Sherman and raised a suspicious eyebrow. "I suppose you were speeding?"

Sherman hung his head and nodded.

"Well then," his friend said, "Annie must have gotten your attention. Seems to me you had better do like she told you and slow down from now on."

Yes, indeed. There was no doubt about it. Sherman had gotten the message—loud and clear. His driving was safer and saner after that. In fact, he even traded in his flashy red sports car for a more sedate, sensible model.

Sherman also felt beholden to Annie for the important lesson she had taught him. He often drove that very portion of

road hoping to see Annie so that he could thank her person-
ally for teaching him such a valuable lesson.

But since he was no longer breaking the speed limit, he
never saw the ghost again.

The Snipe and the Bear

The following trickster tale from East Tennessee involves the bane of every young boy who ever joined a troop of Boy Scouts and embarked on his first camping trip—the infamous snipe hunt. Whether or not the story is true I cannot say. Considering, however, the personal experiences I have had with snipe hunts, I would have no doubts the possibility exists that it is true. Here is the tale of a snipe hunt gone bad, as it was told to me:

Let me start by saying that the snipe is a very real bird, in spite of vicious rumors to the contrary. Just because the long-legged beasties refuse to run into an open gunnysack when some fool is shining a flashlight on the opening and yelling, "Here snipe! Here snipe!" doesn't mean that they don't exist.

True snipes are shore birds and do not live in the woods. However, that established fact doesn't prevent generations of rookie Boy Scouts from hunting them, from the forests of Maine to California—especially when led on such excursions by older, more insidious scouts.

I went on my first and last snipe hunt during my first camping trip with the Boy Scout troop that I had joined a few months before in Erwin, Tennessee. The month was February. It was so cold on top of Spivy Mountain that the water in our canteens froze between gulps.

After dinner, the dozen or so hearty souls on the overnight—our scoutmaster had the good sense to stay home and send his assistant instead—were busily drawing straws seeing what shifts we would take for fire watch. Night had already fallen. The sky was clear and the stars were out. I drew the three-to-four a.m. shift. I thought that I might crawl into my sleeping bag and get a head start on a good night's sleep. But, alas, it was not to be.

One of the First-Class scouts—a haughty and pushy individual that the rest of the scouts had dubbed "Fearless Leader"—suddenly piped up and suggested that new scouts needed the experience of going on a snipe hunt. My buddy Reggie Albright was all for the adventure. I, on the other hand, would have rather stayed by the fire where it was warm. I told him so.

"Come on, you big yellow belly," he chided, his eyebrows drawing together. At eleven years old, Reggie had eyebrows like a gorilla.

"I'm not a yellow belly," I insisted.

Reggie ignored me. Instead, his hand reached for one of the gunnysacks the older boys had brought for the occasion.

"You and Reggie work together," our Fearless Leader told me. Then he sniggered, "You two make a good team."

"What do we do?" I asked.

"Nothing to it," the older boy answered. "One of you hold the sack open and the other shine a flashlight on the front of it. Then you call, 'Here snipe, snipe.' Snipe are attracted to light and the human voice. They'll run right into the sack. Then we'll all have roasted snipe tomorrow for breakfast."

I figured if snipes were that dumb they deserved to end their days in a stew pot.

The older boys led the three pairs of novice snipe hunters into an adjoining woods, about three hundred yards from camp. Fearless Leader took the gunnysack from Reggie's hand. Then he knelt down on the ground and opened the top of the bag, the bottom of the opening resting on a crackling carpet of last summer's leaves. "Like this," he said, looking up. "Hold it like this, then shine your flashlight on the opening."

"And call, 'Here snipe, snipe'?" I asked.

"That's right," he said as he stood and returned the bag to Reggie's eager grasp.

"By the way," Reggie asked, "what exactly does snipe taste like?"

"Chicken," our leader replied without hesitation.

The three teams of snipe hunters were spaced about two hundred feet apart in kind of a rough semicircle in the woods. Fearless Leader's parting words as he left to return to camp were, "Good luck, scouts. Do us proud." I wondered why he and the older scouts didn't join us on the hunt.

"I'll hold the flashlight and the sack," I suggested. "You do the calling."

"Suits me," Reggie replied.

For the better part of a half hour we squatted in the woods, waiting for a snipe to dash into our sack. In the distance we heard the other two teams calling their quarry. I was getting cold, but Reggie was determined. He wasn't about to report to camp empty-handed.

An hour later even Reggie was feeling the chill. We had just decided to give up, when we heard a roar and a scream to our left—then hysterical shouting.

I dropped the sack and hightailed it over to the commotion. Reggie was hard on my heels. When we arrived, we saw another Tenderfoot scout sprawled unconscious on the ground. Bending over him in the darkness was a ratty-looking bear.

"He's dead!" a terrified voice cried. "You killed him!"

The bear took off its head. It was Fearless Leader in a furry costume.

"You killed him deader than a doornail," the frenzied lad continued as he frantically shook his partner.

"He's not dead," the bear/Fearless Leader said nervously. "He's just fainted."

"What were you trying to do, sneaking up on us that way?" the young fellow demanded to know.

By now the rest of the camp had joined us in the woods.

The assistant scoutmaster looked at his unconscious charge on the ground, emitted a stifled groan, and shook his head. He stooped beside the prostrate scout and lifted both his legs. "Somebody get me something to prop these up," he ordered.

I looked around and saw a log lying nearby.

"Put it under his legs," the assistant barked. Then he looked up at Fearless Leader. "Take that costume off and give it to me," he said.

"I'm only wearing skivvies underneath," Fearless Leader answered.

"Good," the assistant replied. "It'll teach you a lesson."

Fearless Leader did as he was told. He was right. Except for a skimpy pair of briefs, he was as naked as the day he was born.

The assistant scoutmaster spread the heavy bear costume over our fallen comrade, bear head resting on his chest. Ten minutes later he came to. The first thing he saw was the bear head staring him in the face. He screamed, sprang to his feet, and, before we could offer an explanation, he fled into the woods.

The assistant turned to Fearless Leader and scowled. "Now you and your buddies go out there and get him."

"Then may I please have my costume? It's cold."

"Nothing doing. Put that thing on and you'll just scare him again."

A half hour later the older scouts returned to camp, an hysterical young scout in tow. He was not afraid anymore. In fact, he was laughing like a hyena. The other boys had told him about the costume and the chilly pay back that Fearless Leader had received at the hands of the assistant scoutmaster.

Fearless Leader was so cold that his teeth were chattering. It's a wonder he didn't catch his death, but he didn't. He crawled into his sleeping bag, zipped the cover over his head, and refused to come out until morning. During my fire watch later that night, I glanced over at the sleeping bag every once in a while and couldn't help but notice that it continued to visibly shake all through my watch.

That was the last time anyone in our troop ever organized a snipe hunt. I heard that when the assistant told our scoutmaster what had happened, he hit the ceiling and decreed that nonsense like that would cease before someone had a heart attack.

NOTE: *Trickster tales, as I said before, abound in folk literature. Folks dressing up as monsters or spirits sometimes find themselves outwitted. But sometimes good can result from the masquerade. Take for example this tale from New Mexico, as it was told by Volney Potter to a WPA writer in 1937:*

Holiaro's grandfather Moreno was a man who believed in being prepared, so he had portholes made in his private fort and stocked it with plenty of food, firearms, and ammunition. The rope ladder leading to the roof could be used by the inmates of the house, then pulled up and concealed. After getting the members of his household safely inside, the cunning old Spaniard would follow them and lock the trap door, which was a clever arrangement running the full length of the roof, defying detection by the keenest eyed Indian on the warpath.

One evening—it was just about sunset, so Holiaro told me— Moreno was warned that the Indians were going to make a raid on his place. Moreno immediately summoned his family and servants, telling them to make haste and enter the fort, for the Indians would soon be upon them. Finally the moon came up. Some of the servants stationed at the portholes reported that they saw shadowy forms skulking behind the trees across the road. Presently another outlook reported that the skulking forms were Indians; of that he was quite positive, for they had built a fire and, as was their custom, formed a circle around it. He then reported that they seemed to be holding a council.

The council held by the Indians must have been of short duration, for following the report the Indians sent forth a blood-curdling whoop and charged Moreno's fort. Six rifles in the hands of six Spaniards exploded through the portholes, and six braves hit the dust. The remaining Indians looked at their dead brothers in amazement and returned the fire. Moreno figured that their next move would be the hurling of firebrands to set the house on fire and burn the inmates. All the time, more Indians kept coming and increasing the circle around the fire. Moreno knew that the Indians were so superstitious that the least thing with a supernatural trend would have more power to drive them away than a thousand armed men.

Along about midnight the Indians piled more mesquite on the fire and started to dance around it, singing the weird uncanny notes of the death song, working themselves into that frenzy which I have been told preceded a massacre. Suddenly some of them slowed down in the dance to stare at something on the roof of the fort. Others followed suit. Then pandemonium broke loose. With screams of terror they fled in a body, and no wonder. The cause of their fright was a ghost so tall that it seemed to meet the sky, with eyes as black as coal and as big as saucers. After the Indians left, old Moreno, who had been lying on the flat of his back juggling a ten-foot viga wrapped in a sheet, let it fall to the roof of the fort with a thud.

The Face in the Water

Is it possible that ghosts sometimes need the help of the living? Could be. I offer into evidence the following tale.

Anyone with a lick of common sense knows that the Nolichucky River is the wrong place for swimming. The river is one insidious trap of undertows, deep holes, and unpredictable currents. Yet not a summer goes by without at least three or four drownings reported in the newspapers—the foolhardy continue to swim in its waters, and fishermen still wade into the stream too far for safety.

Not surprisingly, ghosts of the drowned abound along the Nolichucky. The specter of a nude young woman, for instance, is sighted often—always without warning. She floats noiselessly from the woods, across a sandy bar, and into the water where she disappears beneath the rippling surface.

Legend tells of a young lady and her boyfriend who went on a moonlight swim in the Nolichucky River one night. She was caught in an undercurrent and was swept beneath an overhanging rock, where she drowned. Rescuers mistakenly believed the young woman was carried downstream by the strong current, so it was a week or two before her body was finally discovered.

Is it her ghost we see, floating out of the woods and disappearing beneath the Nolichucky? So-called "ghost logic" dictates that real ghosts follow a pattern of behavior, unchanged from sighting to sighting. If this is correct, then the unfortunate woman's ghost operates according to the program.

Another Nolichucky ghost is that of a fisherman who waded out too far in search of the wily trout. Since the waters of the Nolichucky are generally rather murky, he quickly lost sight of the bottom, misstepped, and fell into a deep hole. Water poured into his waders, his feet hit the sandy bottom of the abyss, and he stayed there.

Several years afterward a convoy of white-water rafts was drifting downstream when the passengers sighted a lone fisherman standing in the stream. They waved and he waved back. Then, suddenly, he disappeared beneath the water.

The leader of the expedition, knowing all too well the unpredictable nature of the river, thought the man had stepped into a deep hole. When he failed to surface, the leader turned his canoe and headed back to the spot where the fisherman was last seen—and still had not surfaced.

Now in a thorough panic, the leader dove into the water to rescue the man. The river was relatively clear that day and the young fellow could see about five feet in front of him. He had been right. There was a hole.

Down he swam, but there was no sign of the fisherman. Had he washed away with the current? The young guide

glanced at the sandy bottom which was rapidly coming up towards him. There in the sand, grinning up at him, was a human skull!

The rafting guide nearly drowned in his sudden panic. He turned and shot up toward the surface, made his way to the shore, and crawled up on the rocks where he lay trembling for a long time.

In due course the guide's grisly find was reported to the police. Divers found a complete skeleton, most of it buried in the sand at the bottom of the hole. And they found something else—a set of rubber waders and a creel—half-rotted reminders of a past tragedy.

When the bones of the victim were finally buried, with all the usual ceremony attendant to the dead, the ghost of the fisherman was never seen again. Perhaps his many appearances were a cry for attention—"Hey, you. This is where I drowned. Come and get my body and give it a proper burial, and I'll trouble you no more!"

And true to its word, it never did.

The Night Creature

This is a variation on the legend of the infamous "Jersey Devil," and just goes to prove that the plot of many ghost lore stories never changes substantially. (I have retold the "Jersey Devil" legend at the end of this story for those of you who may not have heard it.) Locations may vary, but the story remains essentially the same. This tale is from Sevier County.

A thick woods, located in southern Sevier County, is rumored to be the stomping grounds of a terrible half-human beast that slinks through the underbrush in search of a human companion. The creature is said to approach unwatchful travelers, walking through the woods alone, late at night. He makes no noise as he treads on dry leaves underfoot or passes bushes or branches. The victim is unaware of the danger until the monster is upon him.

The creature taps the person on the shoulder to get his attention. The traveler wheels around and sees a monster more horrible than anything he could ever imagine—and immediately dies of fright!

How did this hideous creature come to be? As the old folks tell it, there was once a witchy woman living out in the woods. She was said to be able to cure the sick of all kinds of afflictions, and to mix potions that could make a dry cow give milk or freshen a dry well. This woman had many, many children. The problem was that she hated kids. When she was expecting her thirteenth one, she cursed it and said that it should go to the devil. It did. Shortly after his birth the baby crawled out of the woman's front door, into the woods, and was adopted by a pack of wolves.

As he grew, the cursed child became even too horrible for the wolf pack, and they banished him from their den. So the child grew up in the forest alone, becoming even more ugly as time went on. Eventually he became so grotesque that nothing could stand the sight of him and live. Flowers wilted as he passed. Trees turned from bright green summer colors to winter's brown in an instant. A person could tell where the creature had walked by the dead grass left in his wake.

Although the Night Creature was horrible to see, he had the nature of a kind and gentle person. One night he found a wounded squirrel on the trail and took it to his cave to care for it. He was careful, however, to put the squirrel in an out-of-the-way place so that it would not catch sight of its benefactor. Unfortunately the little animal wandered out into the cave just as the Night Creature was returning from his nightly forage. The squirrel took one look at the horrible monster and died on the spot.

More than anything, the Night Creature wanted human companionship. His loneliness was almost unbearable. Every once in a while a traveler would pass by the monster's cave and the Night Creature would try to greet him. The result was always the same. The stranger would take one look at the monster's horrible face and die of fright. But this did not stop the Night Creature. He tried again and again but everyone he tried to talk to suddenly died.

A farmer was walking home from a Sunday prayer meeting at his local church late one night. There was a full moon, and its dim light filtered through the summer foliage, creating patches of pale yellow light and deep shadow on the forest floor.

The first unusual thing the farmer noticed was that the night birds all stopped their singing. *Odd*, he thought to himself. *Not a single sound can be heard in the woods—not even the usual frogs and crickets.*

Suddenly he felt something tap him on the shoulder. He turned but luckily was looking down. He saw only a pair of feet—scaly, green, and horrible. The farmer had heard about the Night Creature, so he knew if he looked into the creature's face he was done for.

The farmer turned around quickly and began running with all his might. When he got home he raced into the house and told his wife about the close call he had just had with the Night Creature. Being a practical woman, the wife didn't believe him.

The man sat down in front of the fire to catch his breath. His wife continued her cleaning. For some reason she glanced at the window. Her eyes widened with fright. She screamed and fell dead on the floor. Her startled husband turned toward the window just in time to see a huge brown shape disappear. He knew right away what had happened. The Night Creature, in an insistent effort to make friends, had followed him home, and his unfortunate wife had seen the horrible face peering at her through the window.

As far as is known, this man was the only person who lived to tell about his encounter with the Night Creature. It is a shame that the same thing could not be said for his unbelieving wife.

So if you are in southern Sevier County, walking through a certain patch of woods late one night, and something taps you on the shoulder, don't turn around. Run away as fast as you can. And when you finally get home, stay away from all the windows. The thing behind you may be the Night Creature trying to make friends. And he may follow you home.

If you run and hide, you'll be all right. If you are unfortunate enough to look into the horrible face, it will be the last thing you will ever see.

NOTE: *Now, as promised, here are a few facts about the famous "Jersey Devil." There are many versions of the origins of the Jersey Devil, but this is my favorite. Like the Night Creature of Tennessee, the Jersey Devil of the pine lands of New*

Jersey is a cursed child.

There once was a Mrs. Shrouds of Leeds Point who had so many children that she wished that her next one would be a devil. When the child was born, it was horribly misshapen. She kept it in the house so that no one in the neighborhood would ever see it. One night the child began to flap its arms, which turned into wings, and it flew out of the chimney.

In the past 260 years or so the Jersey Devil has been sighted by many people, including Commodore Stephen Decatur (who shot cannonballs at it as it flew across the sky) and the brother of Napoleon Bonaparte. In 1909, the Jersey Devil made an appearance at the farm of Mr. and Mrs. Nelson Evans of Gloucester who watched from their front window as the creature cavorted for a full ten minutes. Mr. Evans described the creature thus:

"It was about three-feet-and-a-half high, with a head like a collie dog and a face like a horse. It had a long neck, wings about two feet long, and its back legs were like those of a crane, and it had horse's hooves. It walked on its back legs and held up two short front legs with paws on them."

When Mr. Evans opened the window and told the critter to shoo, he said that the thing turned and barked at him. Then it flew away.

Sometimes the Jersey Devil is not seen at all—only its cloven footprints. Whatever the thing is—if it be fact or myth—the Jersey Devil is still seen and stories of sightings abound in New Jersey folklore. One thing is certain, though. No one is known to have ever dropped dead by looking at it.

Squeezer

Are you afraid of the bogeyman? Is there something under your bed at night? Do noises scare you after you turn out the lights? Of all childhood fears, nothing quite matches that mysterious something which lurks in the shadows of your room, waiting to pounce on you. It has many names. Most people know the creature as the bogeyman. However, the name of the horror in the following story is Squeezer.

Ever hear of Squeezer?

Do you mean to sit there and tell me that you've never met Squeezer on those cold, dark nights when you're alone in your room with nothing to keep you company but your imagination?

Lots of people have heard of Squeezer. A few have even seen him—before it was too late.

Squeezer is just a little fellow—maybe three or four inches high. But his arms are enormous. They're long enough to wrap themselves completely around a person...maybe two or three times.

Little Squeezer has huge muscles in his arms. So when he hugs your body, he squeezes the life right out of you. That's why they call him "Squeezer."

Now, I happen to know of a person who has seen Squeezer. It all happened when Jeannie was about twelve years old. A friend was staying with her that night. They had watched television until almost eleven o'clock. Now both were dead tired.

By 11:30, both were sound asleep. That was when Jeannie felt something at her feet. At first she thought that the cat had crawled in bed with them. She raised up on her arm to take a look, but she saw right away that it wasn't the cat. A pair of enormous bony hands were reaching up on the bed.

Jeannie started to scream but the sound caught in her throat. Just then her friend woke and sat up in bed. She saw the hands, too. Both watched breathlessly as a head appeared—tiny, green. Little beady eyes were set deep in the skull. Pointed ears grew from the side of its head.

Its arms were enormous, much too long for its body. The hands were huge.

Jeannie did the first thing she could think of in a situation like that. She grabbed a baseball bat and started bashing the creature with all her might.

"Ouch! Ouch! Stop it!" the little creature screamed.

"Get out of this bed," Jeannie shouted. "Get back into that crack that you crawled out of!"

"I will, if you quit beating me over the head!"

Jeannie stopped and lowered the bat. She studied the little creature in the half-light of her bedroom.

"What are you, anyway?"

"I'm your worst nightmare," the creature said menacingly.

"You don't look very scary to me."

Jeannie put the bat on the bed, close enough that it was handy should she need it again. The little creature slowly raised to its full height, still protecting itself with its huge hands. It looked up at the two girls.

"Are you going to hit me again?" it asked.

"Not if you behave yourself," Jeannie answered.

The little creature frowned. "You know, you're not supposed to be acting this way," it said. "You're supposed to be all frightened and screaming and stuff like that!"

"We suppose you're disappointed?"

"A little."

"Who, or what, are you, anyway?"

"My name is Squeezer."

"Wheezer?" Jeannie's friend asked.

"Squeezer!"

What kind of a name is that?" she asked.

"Squeezer is what I do for a living. I squeeze people."

"With arms like that, I don't doubt it," Jeannie said. "Why do you squeeze people?"

"Because I've always done it that way," the creature replied. "It's a tradition—like eating Thanksgiving turkey or hanging up stockings for Christmas. Don't ask such silly questions."

"I can't help it," Jeannie growled. "I'm just a silly person. After all, here we are—peacefully sleeping—and we're suddenly awakened by a two-bit doofus who crawls out from under the bed and claims to be second cousin to the bogeyman. I get real silly when things like this happen."

"Like when your shoes catch fire?" Jeannie's friend asked.

"Exactly!" Jeannie replied.

Squeezer frowned. "Stop this. Stop making fun of me."

"Well, what do you want us to do?"

"You could try screaming or something."

"We're all screamed out. We watched a Freddy Krueger movie earlier this evening."

"I'll tell you what, Jeannie," her friend suggested. "Maybe we could break out into a cold sweat and start shaking or something. Maybe that would make Doofus happy."

"SQUEEZER!"

"Whatever."

Squeezer was getting more frustrated by the moment. These two girls were not cooperating at all. They should be frightened, cowering beneath the covers—instead, they were refusing to take him seriously. He felt like punching both of them in the nose. True to his nature, Squeezer refused to give up.

"I'm going to squeeze you anyway!" Squeezer declared.

"Oh no you don't!" the two girls said in chorus as they both lunged at him. Jeannie grabbed one enormous arm and her friend the other. Both knew right away that they had underestimated Squeezer's strength.

Squeezer tried to shake the girls loose, but they held on for dear life, bouncing off the walls and the ceiling and making a terrible ruckus.

Jeannie's father stormed into the room a moment later and found his daughter and her friend sprawled out on the bed, holding on to something under the pillow.

"What's all the noise about?" he demanded to know.

"We caught the bogeyman," Jeannie said, out of breath.

Jeannie's father pulled the pillow away. His daughter and her friend were grasping each other's arms. "It looks more like you caught each other," he observed crustily.

The two girls looked at each other in amazement. Jeannie turned to her father. "I tell you, we caught the bogeyman."

Her father shook his head. "Don't you think you two girls are a little old for this?" he asked disgustedly. "Now get under the covers and be quiet. Me and your mother are trying to get some sleep."

Jeannie's father closed the door and once again the room was in darkness.

"Do you think he'll come back?" Jeannie's friend asked.

"My father?"

"No, dork. The bogeyman."

"Not likely," Jeannie replied confidently. "We gave him a pretty rough time. Let's go to sleep. I'm tired. He's not coming back."

The two girls rolled over and pulled the covers up over them. Soon they fell asleep, this time a bit deeper than before because all the activity had worn them out.

A half hour later, a pair of claw-like hands appeared at the foot of the bed. Squeezer was back. Then another set appeared—then another. This time Squeezer was taking no chances.

This time he had brought plenty of help.

The Haunted Railroad Crossing

Halloween is the time for witches, spooks, and other denizens of the netherworld to rise up and cavort among the living. Strange and terrifying things are said to happen on this night, even though it is considered a holiday by many. At the same time, perfectly normal people do strange things on this night. Here's a tale from Middle Tennessee about one such instance and its bizarre consequences.

At Florence Road and Highway 70, just west of Murfreesboro, there is a dangerous railroad crossing that was once the site of a tragic event. The crossing there, in fact, has been the site of numerous accidents. And as if to punctuate its notoriety, there is even a graveyard in plain sight of the crossing as a grisly reminder. But on this particular Halloween night twenty years ago, what happened was no accident. It was an out-and-out suicide!

Near the crossing there is a tavern where the locals gathered every Saturday night for a bit of partying. Every Halloween night there was always a big bash. People would come from miles away just to while away All Hallows' Eve with potent drink and boisterous music.

One Halloween a young man took his girlfriend to the bar for a little adult refreshment and some serious partying. Sometime during the course of the evening, he discovered—

to his dismay—that she was a married woman. Still he loved her very much and demanded that she leave her husband and marry him. She refused. All night long they stood at the bar arguing, and their angry words were heard by many, many people.

Eventually the young man, all argued out, swore that he would jump in front of a train at the nearby crossing if his girl-friend didn't get a divorce from her husband and marry him instead. Of course, the woman didn't believe that he would do such a thing and dared him to carry out his threat.

Almost immediately the young man left the bar with some of the revelers—most of them well into their cups—following him. What happened a few minutes later instantly sobered the multitude.

A train whistle was heard in the distance. As the locomotive approached, the young man strode purposefully toward the tracks. Now the locomotive headlight became visible. The diesel horn sounded its warning as the train approached the crossing. Then, to the horror of everyone gathered, the young man walked directly into the path of the train.

No body at all could be found after the train passed. Had the young man's body been taken far down the tracks by the engine and never found? Or did the young man fake his own death? No one knows for sure, because the young man was never seen again!

According to local legend, every Halloween night a ghostly figure is said to jump in front of a passing train at that very crossing. But when the train passes, no body is ever found. One witness that I contacted said that he was driving by the crossing one Halloween night when he saw a man jump in front of a passing train.

"I stopped and got out of the car, just in case," he told me. "But I had no doubt I had seen this guy's ghost. Some of my friends have seen the same thing on other nights. There's no doubt about it. He's still there and still jumping in front of trains. You'd think, being a ghost and all," he said with a chuckle, "that he'd have better things to do with his time."

Bloody Jack

Ghosts guarding, or knowing the secret of, buried treasure is a common motif in folklore. This Middle Tennessee tale is one of my favorites.

On a high plateau in Cumberland County, a ghastly creature guards a hidden treasure and terrorizes everyone with whom he comes into contact. The specter (if the monster can be called a ghost at all) is tall, gaunt, and covered with blood. In life he was said to be an itinerant farrier who traveled from farm to farm shoeing horses. In death, he is known as the infamous "Bloody Jack."

How did Bloody Jack reach his present state of affairs? Early in 1796 Tennessee was about to become a new state— its proud residents were filled with hope and promise for the future. Jack had fought in the Revolutionary War and, as payment for his military services to the state of North Carolina (which owned the territory at the time), had been granted a parcel of land near the new settlement of Nashboro. But Jack was not likely to settle down and become a farmer. There was too much new country to see—too many things to do. So he gave his land to his brother who was more of a farmer than he would ever be, and Jack set off with a pack mule to ply his trade as a farrier.

For years he traveled through the Cumberland Mountains, visiting each farm he encountered and asking if there were mules or horses to be shod. Shoeing was difficult for the farrier and dangerous for the animal. A person really had to know what he was doing; one false move and the animal would be lamed for life. Jack had the skill of a surgeon when it came to shoeing horses. His hammer drove the nails true, and after twenty years of work he had not injured a single animal.

Jack's skill was known and respected throughout Middle Tennessee. He never lacked for business and, as a result of his labors, he became quite wealthy. The lack of banks on the frontier, however, forced Jack to carry his gold with him wherever he went. Naturally trusting of everyone, it didn't bother him that he might be a sitting duck for robbers. Besides, years of hard, backbreaking work had made Jack as strong as an ox. He felt sure that he could easily defeat anyone who would dare rob him of his gold.

One day, as he was traveling over an especially isolated section of trail, he encountered three burly men who had made camp next to a small stream. They invited him to share a haunch of venison that was roasting over their fire. Jack was hungry and readily agreed.

His three new companions seemed friendly enough. In fact Jack thought that he might know one of them.

"Yes," the man replied. "I remember you. My name's Anderson. You came to my daddy's farm about two years ago and shoed a couple of his horses and a mule. Did a right good job, too."

Jack smiled pleasantly as he bit into his portion of the meat.

The other two men glanced at each other, a strange gleam in their eyes.

Anderson continued, "I remember that day very well. Daddy said you asked a lot of money for your work, but after it was over he said it was well worth it."

Jack was proud of his work and was not afraid to say so. "A good job always calls for higher wages," he said as he chewed. "Been doin' that kinda thing for some time now."

Anderson smiled. Then he said, "I guess you got quite a

poke saved up by now."

Jack nodded. "Weighs almost as much as my tools," he answered proudly while nodding toward his mule.

"Should put it in a bank or somethin'," Anderson said smiling. "I hear-tell a new one's opened up in Nashboro. Otherwise you might get yourself robbed and there would be no one around to help you. You never know who might be travelin' these trails."

"It'll be all right," Jack replied, looking up from his meal. He noticed that Anderson's two companions were no longer sitting in their places by the fire. At almost the same moment he felt a strong arm grab him around the neck and pull him back. He dropped his venison.

Anderson leaped to his feet and joined the other men who were now stabbing Jack over and over again with their long knives. Blood squirted from Jack's chest and neck as the men stabbed him again and again!

Finally Jack was dead, his body nothing more than a bloody, lifeless lump of clay lying on the ground. The three men stood up, breathing heavily. Then Anderson walked over to Jack's mule and removed the pack from the animal's back and carried it over to the fire. The men could not help but be impressed at the large amount of gold inside. When they counted it out, it came to just over a thousand dollars—a small fortune in those days.

You have heard it said that there is "honor" among thieves. But the sight of all that gold suddenly became too much for Anderson. Greed overcame him. He wanted all the gold for himself!

When Anderson glanced at his companions, he could see from their expressions that they were each thinking the same thing. Suddenly the men began lunging at each other with their still-bloody knives, but Anderson proved to be the better fighter. In no time at all he had dispatched all the competition for Jack's gold.

Now there were three bloody bodies on the ground and one very rich man, very much alive. Anderson reached for the sack of gold and placed it on his own horse. Just as he finished breaking camp, he heard a twig snap behind him. He turned around. There, standing not twenty feet away, was the bloody figure of Jack. His eyes were rolled back in his head and only the whites were showing. His hair was all matted and stringy with blood and dirt. He reached out two bony hands in Anderson's direction.

"Give me back my gold!" the apparition croaked.

Anderson's horse took one look at Bloody Jack and bolted into the woods, the sack of gold still tied on his back. The horrified murderer took off right behind his terrified horse, trying to catch up.

An hour later, Anderson found the horse, which had stepped into a hole and had broken his leg and was lying on the forest floor in horrible agony. Anderson didn't even pause to put the animal out of his misery. He quickly untied the bag of gold from the horse's back and slung it over his shoulder. Then he started off.

Anderson had not gotten fifty feet when Bloody Jack stepped out from behind a tree.

"I want my gold!" Bloody Jack wailed.

Anderson took off running in the opposite direction. Again he had not gotten more than a few yards when Bloody Jack popped out from behind a boulder. "I want my gold," he groaned.

Anderson screamed in terror and began running off in an entirely different direction, this time along the bank of a small stream. Suddenly Bloody Jack rose up out of the water, his bloody hands extended. "I want my gold!" he screamed.

With a holler Anderson turned and ran through the woods, trying to outdistance the ghost that was now chasing him. He ran as hard as he could, occasionally tripping over branches and rocks in his path. At every turn he was confronted by Bloody Jack, his hands outstretched. "I want my gold," the ghost hissed, over and over again. And every time Jack would appear, Anderson changed direction, all the time getting deeper and deeper into the woods.

With every step Anderson thought that his lungs would burst for want of air. Still he had to get away from the ghost.

The sack of gold, slung over his back, was getting heavier and heavier.

Suddenly the slope of the forest floor changed—he was running downhill. Anderson's pace quickened. Surely now he would get away. Anderson glanced over his shoulder. Bloody Jack was right behind him. Anderson suddenly felt the ground leave his feet. He was poised in midair, a few feet past the brim of a high cliff. Panic seized him. He looked down as a sharp outcropping of rock, several hundred feet below, rushed up at him.

Then oblivion.

It is said that Bloody Jack recovered his bag of gold from Anderson's smashed body—after the murderer had fallen over that cliff—and buried it for safekeeping somewhere in the forest near the present-day town of Cookeville, though no one knows for sure. The legend of the buried gold, of course, has sent many treasure seekers into the woods to search. And for nearly every treasure hunter who has entered those woods, another strange tale of Bloody Jack's ghost has come out.

Eyewitnesses report seeing a bloody man, dressed in old-fashioned clothing, sitting on top of a rock, just staring at them. Most know the story of Bloody Jack and, naturally, they assume his figure is sitting on top of the treasure, guarding it. Understandably, few approach the spot. No one wants to share Anderson's terrible fate.

The gold Anderson stole from Jack is, of course, certainly worth a lot more now than it was worth then. But few treasure hunters want to risk an encounter with Bloody Jack.

As Anderson discovered much to his horror, you can't fight a very determined ghost.

The Ghost of the Sherrod Library

I'd like to tell a tale that I've told before. It was originally printed in one of my early books. But I think that it is a very good story and deserves another airing.

The so-called "old stacks" in the old Sherrod Library building at East Tennessee State University were tucked away in a nebulous nook behind the brightly lit reference room. Here were kept books that had limited circulation—usually older editions and outdated volumes—but still valuable in specialized research situations.

The old stacks were dark and shadowy, the shelves squeezed close together in a claustrophobic arrangement. Each level of the old stacks was reached by a narrow, winding staircase that looked like part of the set from a horror movie. Even without the resident ghost said to lurk in the old stacks, that part of the Sherrod Library could get very spooky. It was a place where your imagination could very easily get the best of you.

Students and staff claimed that an unseen presence was sometimes felt in the bowels of the old stacks, as if someone was looking over the browser's shoulder. The feeling was strongest on the lower floor.

Campus legend identifies the ghost as a former librarian, a no-nonsense matron still jealously guarding her books. Richard Lyons, a former student at ETSU, said that every time he went into the old stacks, he could feel someone watching him.

"The feeling wasn't frightening or malevolent," he said. "But it was like someone was concerned—like they thought you were going to steal something and they were watching to make sure that you didn't."

One staff member, who said she spent a great deal of time in the old stacks, told me this story of her encounter with the ghost. She claimed to have actually seen it!

"It was during Christmas break," she began. "Nothing much is happening in the library then. Most of the students are enjoying their vacation and only a few diehard graduate students use the library. Things are pretty quiet and the library is open on limited hours.

"I decided that I would go down into the old stacks and nose around. I often do that. You never know what kind of treasure you might uncover. I remember once that I found an old chronology of music down there—a book that kept me fascinated for weeks.

"Well, I walked through the reference room, turned on the lights in the old stacks, and walked down the winding iron stairs to the lower level. I hadn't been down there but a few minutes when I got this feeling that someone was behind me. I turned around but didn't see anything.

"I went back to my searching and a few minutes later I had the same feeling. I turned around again, but nothing was there.

"I had heard stories about the old stacks being haunted, but I didn't believe in ghosts—at least, then I didn't. I was in the old stacks about fifteen minutes before I found a book that I wanted to read. I put it under my arm, turned, and began walking toward the staircase. Suddenly I saw a figure slowly descending the stairs.

"At first I thought it was another worker. Well, if it had been another worker, her legs were missing!

"What I saw was the torso of a woman, dressed in an old-fashioned, high-neck maroon dress, gliding down the stairs. My blood turned to ice. I could see her face clearly. She had a very stern expression and was wearing old-fashioned, wire-rimmed glasses. Her hair was tied back in a tight bun.

"The figure stopped at the bottom of the stairs and just floated there for a second or two, looking at me. I was speechless. I couldn't move.

"Then the figure disappeared. I ran up the steps and out of the old stacks as fast as I could. I wasn't going to stay there one more second.

"From then on, I never went into the old stacks again unless someone else was with me!"

Bandy Eyes

You have probably heard stories about summoning up "Candyman" or "The Bell Witch." Now hear the story of "Bandy Eyes," an elusive spirit that some say can be conjured from any mirror. Belief in Bandy Eyes seems to be rather widespread throughout Tennessee, and children from all over the state have told me about their efforts to scare themselves silly by trying to contact it. One young lady, however, told the following tale of how she was chillingly successful in summoning up ol' Bandy Eyes.

I was about ten years old when all of this took place. Our home was in the country—about ten miles from the nearest town of any size. I lived there with my mother and father, two sisters, and three brothers.

As the youngest girl in my family I was, of course, the apple of my daddy's eye. This caused some bad feelings with the rest of my siblings, and they were always trying to put something over on me. I'll have to admit I was extremely gullible, especially when it came to ghost stories.

My brother Adam (he was about twelve at the time) was especially astute at scaring the devil out of me with wild tales. My father was always on his case about that, but he continued anyway. Adam was the one who told me about ol' Bandy Eyes.

Adam said that ol' Bandy Eyes was an evil spirit that lived

in mirrors—somewhere between the glass and the silver backing. Bandy Eyes was a shape-shifter. When a person looked into a mirror, Bandy Eyes could assume the likeness of the person. Most people thought it was their own reflection in the mirror. It wasn't. It was actually Bandy Eyes looking back.

One night Adam told me that Bandy Eyes sometimes showed his true self in the mirror but, in order to do so, one had to call him forth.

"How do you do that?" I asked.

"Nothing to it," Adam whispered. "You hold the mirror in front of your face and say, 'Bandy Eyes, Bandy Eyes, come forth and show your true self to me.' But you have to say it five times—if you dare. Then you'll see Bandy Eyes."

"Let's try it," I said eagerly.

Adam backed up a few steps. "Not me," he said nervously. "I have no intentions of seeing him."

"Did you ever see him before?" I asked.

"Just once, and that was enough! It was the most horrible thing I ever saw in my life—these two horrible eyes staring back at me from the mirror in the place where my real eyes should have been." Then he warned me, "You can call him up if you want to, but whatever you do, don't break the mirror!"

After Adam left my room, I walked over to my bureau and picked up the silver hand mirror that Mom had given me for my birthday. The frame was heavy metal and there were flowers carved all over it. I thought it was the most beautiful mirror in all the world and I could not imagine anything so horrible as Bandy Eyes lurking in it. Still, I was curious and I felt that I had to try to evoke the spirit of the mirror. I took a deep breath and held the mirror up to my face. Then I said, "Bandy Eyes, Bandy Eyes, come forth and show your true self to me."

Adam told me that I would have to say it five times in order for Bandy Eyes to become visible. So four times more I said, "Bandy Eyes, Bandy Eyes, come forth and show your true self to me." After the fifth time nothing happened.

I was mad at my brother Adam. He had obviously put one over on me—again! Well maybe, I thought, I had miscounted and had only said the line four times. I looked back into the mirror and was about to say the words again. What I saw nearly took my breath away.

In the place of my own eyes, there were two others. These were big and round—huge whites with blood-red pupils. It was Bandy Eyes looking directly back at me!

I screamed and dropped the mirror. It hit the floor and the glass shattered into a million pieces. I fled the room and bumped into Adam, who was standing right outside my door. He went sprawling. He leaped to his feet, grabbed my arm, and shouted, "What's the matter with you?"

"Bandy Eyes!" I cried. "He's in the mirror!"

"Let me see," Adam said, nearly dragging me back in the room.

When my brother saw the broken mirror on the floor, he let out a moan and sat down heavily on the bed. "You broke the mirror," he said. "I warned you not to do that!"

"I was scared."

"Well," he said looking up at me, "You've really gone and done it this time. Ol' Bandy Eyes has escaped. It's a good thing that he won't be able to live very long outside the mirror. Just a few years. But while he's around, he'll torment you."

I was really scared now. "What will he do?" I croaked.

"Well, you've heard about people who break mirrors," Adam said sadly. "For seven years now, ol' Bandy Eyes will make sure that you'll have nothing but bad luck! That is his revenge!"

Rap... Rap... Rap...

Ah, yes. The classic haunted house.

How many stories have we heard about houses infested with ghosts? How many books or short stories feature a haunted house as a central motif? It seems that every community has one—an old dilapidated structure, forgotten by time, and allegedly occupied by only the spirits of the dead.

From Maine to Florida, from California to South Carolina, there are stories of haunted houses. Mrs. Rose Williams of Glendale, Long Island, once told WPA writer William Wood: "I can remember a haunted house, a very old frame building where the tenants never remained long. It was owned by a brewer, Frank Eberts, and was said to be the scene of a murder that had been committed years earlier. Many people who sneered at superstition, and voiced their defiance of ghosts, occupied the premises from time to time. They were awakened at night by weird noises and uncanny sounds. Some claimed that they heard shrieks and moans. Those who had most blatantly mocked the supernatural usually were the quickest to seek another residence. Eventually, Mr. Eberts had the house renovated from basement to roof. The old doors and windows were covered up by new lumber, and new doors and windows were made in other places. The effect seemed magical. The 'ghost' apparently had found repose, for the next occupant of the house made no complaint. Finally, Mr. Eberts himself moved in. Two years afterwards, he died; and people said the ghost had returned."

This is one of my favorite haunted house stories that I tell to children every chance I get. I must have heard this tale a hundred times, in all parts of the South, and the content never changes—only the location.

There was once a woman who lived with her husband in a large, white, two-story farmhouse in a remote part of the county. They were so far out in the sticks that their closest neighbor lived over a mile away.

The woman's husband enjoyed the solitude of living in the country. The wife, on the other hand, was not very comfortable so far removed from civilization, especially since her husband sometimes worked late at night at his job as a computer programmer. It was on such a night, when he was gone, that a violent thunderstorm blew out of the southwest and struck that part of the county, causing the failure of both the lights and the phone.

The terrified woman was all alone in the dark old house. She tried to tell herself that she was safe enough and that her husband would return soon. But the notion didn't give her very much comfort.

She glanced at the clock. Eleven p.m.

She lit one of the kerosene lamps she had on hand for just such an emergency and placed it in the middle of the kitchen table. Then she sat down and began nervously munching on some cookies that she had taken from the pantry.

In an hour the storm had passed and it would be just a matter of time until the utilities were restored. As she waited, she heard a faint sound coming from overhead. Rap... Rap... Rap...

What could that be? she asked herself nervously. She knew for sure that there was no one in the house with her. Could it be a mouse?

She heard the sound again. Rap... Rap... Rap...

It sounded like it was coming from the second floor. She shuddered when she suddenly realized that someone was probably in the house with her!

The only weapon available to her was an ancient double-barreled 12-gauge shotgun that her husband used during squirrel season. She found the gun and loaded two shells into the chambers. Then she climbed the steps to the second floor.

The woman searched every nook and cranny but found nothing. She was preparing to return to the first floor when she heard the sound over her head—again!

Rap... Rap... Rap...

She realized with a shudder that the sound was actually coming from the attic!

The attic was one of those cavernous rooms that covered the entire third floor of the structure. It was filled with old furniture, boxes, trunks, and dust. It was dark and shadowy, and the only light source was a single sixty-watt bulb hanging from the ceiling. (Of course, at the present time, the electricity was out.) There were hundreds of places to hide there, and nowhere to run. But there was no way around it now. She had to go into that dark attic to discover what unseen presence was lurking there.

She stood for several moments at the head of the stairs leading to the attic door, gathering her courage. With the shotgun poised under her arm, she started her long climb.

Rap... Rap... Rap...

There it was again. That sound. It was definitely coming from behind the attic door. The woman tensed for a second, then continued her ascent.

Rap... Rap... Rap...

She was halfway up the stairs now, the attic door coming closer by the second.

Rap... Rap... Rap...

Three-quarters of the way. Every muscle in her body was taut. Her mind ran through her plan of attack when she got to the door. She would turn the old-fashioned brown knob with one hand, hold the shotgun in the other, and kick open the door with her foot. That way she thought she might surprise whatever was on the other side and get it before it got her.

Rap... Rap... Rap...

Now she stood poised at the door. Sweat poured from her face. Her finger slowly curled around the shotgun's trigger.

Rap... Rap... Rap...

She reached out for the doorknob. She lifted her foot and...

Rap... Rap... Rap...

...kicked the door open. And there it was—on the other side of the door—staring at her. Horrible!

It was a roll of wrapping paper!

The Mystery of Sensabaugh Tunnel

Haunted lovers' lanes are scattered over the length and breadth of this country. These spark so called "bloody tales from lovers' lanes"—tales of ghosts and inhuman monsters lurking in thick woods, just waiting to pounce on unsuspecting lovebirds. Haunted lovers' lanes have existed for years—from the days of the horse and buggy to the present. The following is the story of one such haunted area. It is unusual in that it involves a man-made structure. Years ago a murder was committed there. Today the ghost of a crying baby haunts the tunnel and wreaks havoc on modern transportation.

Ramshackle Sensabaugh Tunnel, located in Sullivan County, is the kind of place you would probably want to avoid—unless you're in the company of your one true love and are looking for an out-of-the-way place to engage in a little serious necking. The place looks like it's about to fall in at any minute.

And...sometimes at night, the sound of a crying baby echoes through the two-hundred-foot-long concrete tube. Upon investigation, of course, no baby is found! Sensabaugh Tunnel, according to local tradition, however, is very much haunted!

Sensabaugh Tunnel was built in the 1920s. Engineers building a new road thought it was much easier to punch a hole through a rocky ridge than to cut a "V" for a roadbed. It was in this tunnel that a man was supposed to have killed a baby.

One story claims the man was a hobo. One day, while traveling through the area, he stopped at a local house to ask for work in exchange for a meal. The family obliged him.

After chopping some wood, the hobo was invited into the house to eat. Although not rich, the family did have some valuable items scattered around the house. When the hobo attempted to steal a silver cup—an heirloom that had been in the family for years—the husband ran for a pistol.

Not wanting to be shot by the angry man, the hobo grabbed the nearest shield—the couple's baby who was sleeping in a nearby cradle—and ran out the door. The hobo easily outdistanced the father, and when he finally took a breather, he looked at the infant in his arms and decided that the baby would be excess baggage. So he drowned it in the little creek that flows through the tunnel.

I know nothing more of the story nor of the circumstances surrounding the murder, but the eerie memory of the deed lingers on. The sounds of that ghostly baby are often heard today inside the tunnel.

As new, modern roads were built in and around Kingsport, the old road was used only by locals. The tunnel fell into disrepair. Today there are gigantic cracks in the superstructure. Graffiti covers almost every inch of concrete surface, even the high arched ceiling. (Talk about Michelangelo and the Sistine Chapel! One has to wonder how they got up there to paint that ceiling inside the tunnel.) The area around the tunnel has become known as a lovers' lane.

Couples park at Sensabaugh Tunnel to get away from the maddening crowd. And of course, in time-honored tradition, the boys tell the girls wild tales about the history of the tunnel and its resident ghost. Hopefully the girl will get scared and scoot a little closer to her young man.

But there is more to the story than just a murdered baby. The haunting is, as they say in our computer-oriented society, interactive. Tradition has it that when the ghost baby starts to cry, cars won't start. I've talked to at least three people who have had that particular unnerving experience. One young lady was so frightened that she took off running and had put a mile between her and Sensabaugh Tunnel before her boyfriend finally got his auto started and caught up with her!

In mid-October 1998, I was asked by Tim Cable of WJHL-TV in Johnson City to help produced a multi-part series on area hauntings for his show "Cable Country." The plan was to broadcast the series as a special feature during the regular news broadcasts around Halloween. One of the places we visited was Sensabaugh Tunnel. It was there that Tim and his videographer, Doug Counts, had an experience that I'm still laughing about.

Tim Cable is one of those unique characters who you can depend on to do the unexpected. One day, for instance, a fan sent him a humongous stuffed rat and he proceeded to do his entire weathercast with this thing in his hand, using its long skinny tail as a pointer for his weather map. On another occasion Tim was hosting a segment on the covered bridge in Elizabethton and on the possibility that vampires used the bridge as a nesting place. He did the entire segment hanging by his legs from the bridge like a bat!

On this day, Tim and Doug thought it would be clever to stop the WJHL van in the middle of Sensabaugh Tunnel and fake the fact that they couldn't get it started again. Tim hopped out of the van hefting the video camera and began rolling. Doug turned the key ever so slightly and the engine immediately coughed to life.

Once again, Doug turned the ignition ever so slightly. The engine immediately started.

You could almost smell the frustration in the air.

This went on for the better part of fifteen minutes. Doug would try NOT to start the van and the van WOULD start in spite of him. Of course there was nary the sound of a crying baby to be heard. I don't think that Tim and Doug ever did get the shot they wanted.

Maybe the ghost was toying with them, having itself an eerie horselaugh at their antics. Or maybe there is nothing there at all. Who knows?

I do know this, however. Lonely haunted spots, like Sensabaugh Tunnel, are a natural magnet for those searching for a lovers' lane. And as long as Sensabaugh Tunnel stands—from the look of it, it won't be very long—and stories will be told about its resident ghost, the place will continue to attract and its folklore will grow.

And you can take that to the bank!

The Doppelgänger

A doppelgänger is a person's spiritual double. Some folks think that it is the aura or the astral body of a person, somehow detached from the body for a short time. Some actually go so far as to claim that the image in a mirror is actually a person's doppelgänger staring back. No matter what it is, sometimes the appearance of the doppelgänger foretells tragedy. The following is such a tale from West Tennessee—a creepy bit of family lore, two members of which had their own experiences.

Many years ago a young girl was told the legend of the doppelgänger by her German-born mother. "Sometimes," she said, "a person meets his own spiritual double. When he does, it means that he's going to die soon. I heard that Catherine the Great of Russia once saw her spiritual double walking toward her. She was so frightened that she ordered her soldiers to shoot it. Of course, the doppelgänger wasn't harmed, but Catherine died a few hours later."

The little girl took a deep breath and hoped that she would never see her own doppelgänger—ever!

The mother continued. "Now according to my grandfather, on the feast day of St. Mark—every April 24th—a person standing by a church door at midnight will see the doppelgängers of all the people who will die in the coming year as they file into the church."

"Did you ever try that, Mom?" the girl asked.

"Not me," the mother replied. "I was too scared that I would see myself!"

"Then you believe in this?"

"I don't know," the mother replied thoughtfully. Then she smiled. "I'm just not taking any chances."

Now this young girl was very curious. And since April 24th was just a few days away, she made immediate plans to stand vigil outside her family's church and watch for the parade of doppelgängers. Of course, she didn't tell her mother about her plans. She knew that she would not let her go. She would have to sneak out of the house.

On the appointed night the girl kissed her mother and father good night and climbed the steps to her second-story bedroom. Then, at eleven o'clock, she opened her bedroom window, climbed out on the roof of the front porch, shinnied down the trellis, and ran off into the night. Fifteen minutes later she reached the church door.

The night was dark. There was no moon, but the sky was splattered with hundreds of thousands of stars. It was also very chilly. Since there was about a half hour to wait, she was thankful that she had thought ahead and had worn a jacket to ward off the cold. She pulled the fur collar close around her neck. Then she settled down behind a convenient bush.

It wasn't very long before the little girl began shaking all over. She wasn't cold. She was scared! It was almost midnight and she began to have second thoughts about the wisdom of her little excursion. Maybe she would see something that she wasn't supposed to see. Maybe she would find out something that she didn't want to know. Maybe, like her mother had feared, she would see her own doppelgänger in the procession. She decided to get out of there before it was too late.

As she stood up to leave, she saw a faint glow hovering in the church graveyard. Then she could just make out hazy figures approaching. It was too late to run now. She ducked down behind the bush. Her heart was pounding.

The ghostly procession of doppelgängers slowly floated

toward the church door. The girl could make out about a dozen figures. The one in front looked exactly like old man Evans. The little girl knew he had suffered for years from a horrible disease.

Then there came the image of Lorainne Jackson. She was the oldest woman in town. In fact, she was so old that she had forgotten the year she was born.

The next doppelgänger was that of Marvin Stuart, an elderly man. He had owned a grocery store in town for years. When he retired, the business had been taken over by his son. Mr. Stuart was well into his eighties and had been an invalid for several years.

One by one the procession of doubles—doppelgängers— filed into the church. The girl recognized most of them. The town was so small that she knew nearly everyone. Everybody that she had seen was elderly. That was good, she thought. There would be no deaths of young people—at least in the coming year.

The last doppelgänger in the procession was drawing near. The girl had seen more ghosts this night than she ever cared to see again. As soon as the last one passed, she would run for home, slip quietly into her bedroom, and no one would be the wiser.

The final doppelgänger was just passing. The young girl gasped in fright when she looked into its face. She immediately recognized who it was. The last doppelgänger that night was her very own mother!

The young girl's mother was only in her early thirties when she suddenly died two weeks later of a stroke. The girl had not told her what she had seen that night at the church. She had been afraid to—not because she believed the legend of the doppelgänger, but she was afraid that she would be punished for sneaking out that night. Now, with her mother's death, she knew for certain that the legend was true. And she also knew for certain that she would never watch for doppelgängers again!

The little girl grew up—raised by her father—eventually got married, and had children of her own. And, as it was in most families, family lore was passed from mother to daughter. One of the mother's stories was her experience with the doppelgängers years before. Her daughter, of course, enjoyed the story but did not believe it. She was a modern teenager, and stories about ghosts, while entertaining, were not to be taken seriously.

But, like her mother, this modern teenager was curious. One night—on April 24th—she slipped out of the house and walked down to the local church to see if she could see the doppelgängers for herself.

The next morning, at breakfast, she told her mother about her adventure.

"You shouldn't have gone down there," the mother said nervously.

"I beg your pardon," the teenager said. "That's like the pot calling the kettle black!"

Her mother frowned. "Just what do you mean by that, young lady?"

"You were down there at the church yourself. I saw you."

The mother dropped the coffee cup she was holding. It fell to the floor and shattered into bits.

"Mom!" the girl asked. "What's wrong?"

The mother took a deep breath. "I was in this house all night," she said. "I never walked out the door!"

Two weeks later the mother was found dead on the kitchen floor. The doctor said that it was a massive heart attack. But most people—including her teenaged daughter—think that she actually died of fright!

The Ghosts of Apartment 304

Stories of ghosts who actually hurt people are rare. Terrify, yes—abuse, no. This tale from Memphis, however, proves to be the exception to the rule.

Many years ago there was a fancy apartment house that burned down on a very hot Memphis night. All of the residents escaped the flames except a young couple who, under the oddest of circumstances, were burned alive.

The man, people said, was a chronic drunk who abused his wife when in his cups. On this night he had come home in an especially ugly mood and had beaten his wife senseless. Then, having grossly overindulged in strong drink, the man passed out on the bed. About that time flames began in the basement of the apartment house and made their way through the entire building. The next morning the couple's horribly charred bodies were found in the ashes.

A few years passed. A new apartment house was erected on the site of the old building. After it opened it didn't take long for odd events to start happening. There were noises, voices, and other poltergeist activity—especially in the northeast corner of the building. The terrified screams of a woman often erupted in the middle of the night. One of the apartments, in particular, became unrentable because of the abundant activity there. Eventually only those in the direst of circumstances would rent apartment 304.

One person did.

A young single parent with two daughters moved into Apartment 304 several years ago. The woman had just left her husband and, since housing in Memphis was at a premium at the time, she had no choice but to take up residence in the haunted apartment.

Actually, the woman didn't believe in ghosts. Certainly she had heard stories about the strange doings in her new digs, but she had discounted them as mere tales. Her mind was soon to change.

For some reason malevolent ghosts hate cats. The woman had a kitten—the youngest girl's pet. No sooner had the family moved in the first boxes of belongings than the cardboard pet carrier, containing the cat, was snatched from the hand of one of the girls and hurled across the room. The animal, although shaken up, was unharmed.

The woman told her eldest daughter to put the cat in the bathroom and lock the door so the animal wouldn't be underfoot during the rest of the move. After all of the belongings were safely in the apartment, one of the girls was told to retrieve the cat. When she opened the door, she discovered the animal cowering in a corner. When she reached out her hand, the cat raised its back, hissed, and clawed her. It was terrified!

That night, after the girls had been safely tucked into bed, the woman was lying in her own bed. It was about 9:30. Suddenly she thought she heard voices—a man and a woman—arguing. She sat up and looked around the darkened room. She was alone, but the voices continued. The phantom woman began to scream.

Just then the terrified daughters burst into the room. They jumped into their mother's bed and burrowed beneath the covers.

"What's the matter?" their mother asked.

"There's a man in the hallway," the youngest one screamed, "and he ain't got no legs!"

The woman opened the drawer of her nightstand and drew out the loaded .38 she always kept handy in case of intruders. While the girls continued shaking under the covers, she opened the door and peered out into the hallway.

The hall was empty. She searched the rest of her apartment but there was no one there.

The woman returned to her bed. By now the phantom voices had stopped. She tried to tell herself that it had been her imagination. After all, she didn't believe in ghosts. She tried to convince her girls to return to bed, but they begged to sleep with her that night.

An hour later, all three were awakened by the smell of smoke. However, there was no smoke in the apartment and all the smoke alarms were silent. The woman got out of bed and looked down the hallway. It was clear. No smoke could be seen anywhere.

Then the voices started again. The man was shouting—the woman was screaming.

At that moment the girls leaped out of the bed and ran to a corner, holding each other in terror. Just as the woman turned from the doorway, she reeled from the powerful blow of an unseen hand. She lost her footing and fell to the floor.

Her daughters screamed in terror.

The woman had had enough. Grabbing her girls and the cat, she fled the building.

Downstairs, she ran into the manager of the apartment, who had just finished some late night paperwork in his office. When he saw the terrified trio run through the lobby he shouted, "What's wrong?"

"There's a fire," the woman replied as she ran out of the front door. "And there are ghosts in our apartment! One of them hit me."

Of course, there was no fire. The manager knew that. As for the ghosts.... Well, the manager knew about that, too. He also realized he would never see his latest tenant again. She was clearly too terrified to return.

So if you are ever apartment hunting in Memphis and come upon an apartment house, and the manager offers you the empty Apartment 304 at a bargain rate, don't be fooled. Chances are that Apartment 304 is no bargain!

NOTE: *Here is another tale of a haunted apartment taken from the archives of the Work Progress Administration's writers' project of the 1930s. This one is from New York City:*

Not long after we moved (she was then living with a brother) to 117th Street, I had a funny thing happen to me. It was a seven-room apartment, and I had one of the rooms on the street fixed up as a sewing room. The sewing room, bathroom and kitchen were on one side of the hall, the storage room (a small room which she used for trunks and suitcases) and two bedrooms were on the other side. My living room was at the end of the hall and there was a bedroom off from that.

Well, one day I was sitting in the sewing room when I heard a rustle in the hall. It sounded like the swish of a taffeta skirt. I looked up at the door and saw the figure of a woman go past. She had on a black taffeta dress and I didn't see any head. I called out, "Who's there?"

Of course, nobody answered. I jumped up and looked down the hall. Just as the figure reached the door of the living room, it disappeared. I went in and looked around, but I didn't see anything. I went back to the sewing room and picked up my work. I just shrugged my shoulders and said I was seeing things. Nothing else happened like that for a long time. Then one day, a friend was sitting in the sewing room with me, and I heard the rustle again. I looked up and saw the figure again. H. saw it, too. And she said, "Good God, L.! What's that?" I laughed and said, "What's what?" She told me what she had seen. I told her that it was just her imagination, that she had seen a reflection from the street. She insisted that she had seen the headless figure of a woman. She was nervous for about ten minutes, then she quieted down, but she kept insisting that she had seen something. She said that it must have been somebody who had died in the house, and was coming back to look for something. Well, I know that I had seen something, so I said to myself that it must have been a good spirit since it hadn't bothered me, so I didn't worry about it any more while I was in that house.

Crazy George

Tales of tricksters who disguise themselves as ghosts and scare the yell out of the living permeate folklore. Take for example this tale that was told to a WPA worker in the late 1930s by Milledge Richardson of Mulberry Grove Plantation, Florida: "Once there was a joke played that was half believed. Cornelius Brown and some of the boys were returning from church one night. Their way led through a swamp. As they walked they started talking about ghosts, when suddenly in a wet slough on ahead, Brown said three white ghostly figures rose out of the swamp. He called his companions' attention to the sight and they started yelling at the top of their voices, running as fast as they could. One looked back to see if he was followed, jumped a six-foot gate, fell and called for help. When he finally got home he was so frightened he was afterwards sick for six months. The three figures were Reed Pearson, with Sam and Joe Reece, draped in sheets. Cornelius had been told they were going to pull off this stunt, but the others did not know about it and forever afterwards thought they had really seen ghosts in the swamp."

Here is a hair-raising trickster tale from our own Cumberland Plateau where a young man, playing a famous haunt, outsmarts himself.

Those who knew Crazy George are probably all dead now—if they're not, they should be. All this happened almost 150 years ago. Even George, himself, is dead, to be sure, although he is still seen quite frequently walking along his beloved railroad tracks near Cookeville. His ghost, people say, treads the cinders, looking for its head!

"I saw him once, many years ago," an old fellow once told me. "It was the darndest thing. Here was this guy without a head, walking up and down the tracks in the middle of the night. I would have stayed longer, but the girl I was walking home at the time turned and ran away so fast that I had a hard time catching up with her."

Old-timers in Cookeville tell the story this way: When George was young, in the days just before the Civil War, trains were his passion. His fondest ambition was to become a railroad engineer. George would sit by the tracks and watch the old wood-burning locomotives by the hour. Sometimes he would go into the lumberyard and watch as cars were loaded and unloaded. He never tired of watching trains, and constantly badgered the railroad for a job. Finally, just to get rid of the pest, the railroad relented and gave Crazy George a job—not as an engineer, but as a blocker.

Now a blocker was the most dangerous of all jobs on the railroad. Blockers were stationed at various spots along tracks which ran down a steep grade. If the brakes failed on a train, it was the blocker's duty to jam huge blocks of wood under the train wheels to either stop it or slow it down. (These were the days before air brakes, and runaway trains were commonplace.)

As a blocker, one either had a lot to do in a short time, or nothing to do for a long time. More often than not, a blocker would be encumbered with boredom. George was so afflicted one hot day, while on duty, that he fell asleep under a shady tree.

Suddenly he was jerked awake by the frenzied screech of a train whistle. He opened his eyes and saw a train roaring down the mountainside. Still groggy, George leaped to his feet and grabbed one of the big wooden blocks to throw under the train wheels. Unfortunately he got tangled up in his own feet and fell across the tracks, where the heavy engine passed over his neck, decapitating him.

His body was given a Christian burial, but his head was never found. To this day, folks say that the headless ghost of Crazy George walks the rails looking for his head.

The legend of Crazy George, of course, handily lends itself to pranksters. Many a person has pulled the collar of his shirt over his head and has walked the tracks pretending to be George looking for his head. And perhaps this accounts for many of the sightings of George. But does it account for them all?

Folklore is rife with tales of pranksters who outsmart themselves. One such yarn revolves around a young man who decided to assume the role of the headless ghost one Halloween night. He made arrangements with another friend to drive by at the appointed hour with a load of females that they both wanted to scare half to death.

That night at the appointed hour, the young fellow stood beside the lonely stretch of track where, over a hundred years before, Crazy George had lost his head. It was late at night and there were few cars on the road which ran parallel to the track. Then, in the distance, lights appeared.

That must be them, the young man thought to himself. *Time to do my stuff.*

He pulled his shirt collar over the top of his head and was able to see just a tad from between the button-up front. *I hope I don't trip over my own feet,* he thought.

The young man could hear the car approaching now. So he began walking along the track, searching the ground as if looking for his head. As the car passed, barely twenty feet away, he could clearly hear the frenzied screams of the girls from inside the vehicle. Boy, was he pleased with himself! What a laugh he and his friend would have the next day at school.

The two young fellows met the next day, just before lunch. "Brother," the friend said. "Those girls were scared out of their gourd. You should have heard them screaming!"

"I did," the young man laughed. "I heard you as you passed by."

"It took an hour before I got them calmed down again."

"Did you tell them that it was a trick?"

"No, I was afraid to. I think they would've killed me if they found out." Then the friend got a serious expression on his face. "I just have one question. Why did you feel it was necessary to have two Crazy Georges out there last night? One would have been more than enough."

"What on earth are you talking about?" the young man asked, his voice turning into almost a whisper.

"There were two of you out there walking the tracks."

"You're crazy. I was out there by myself."

The friend was silent for a moment. He just stared. Finally the young man asked, "Did the girls also see two?"

The friend nodded. "We all saw two," he said.

The short hairs on the back of the young man's neck raised up like a startled porcupine. The real Crazy George had shown up, too. The shirt over the young man's neck had prevented him from seeing anything but what was directly in front of him. He had been in the company of a real ghost all along and had never known it.

Pap Rises from the Dead

No one likes to think about dying. These days, everyone seems to want to live forever. But, of course, we know that's impossible. However, it doesn't stop us from trying.

That wasn't always the attitude. Back in the days when the great state of Tennessee was being settled, death was a fact of life—accepted stoically by a people who were basically fatalists. They accepted their lot in life, as well as in death. They had no choice. Nutrition was basically unknown. Medicine was primitive. They simply put their faith in God and did the best they could.

The average life span for a person was about thirty-five or forty. For infants, there was a better than even chance they would never see adulthood. One of the main reasons that families were so large in the eighteenth century and early part of the nineteenth was that parents could expect at least fifty percent of their offspring to die before the age of twelve.

The majority of people died during the coldest days of winter—especially the very young and the very old. They fell before all kinds of diseases—pneumonia and other respiratory problems were the most common. Since the ground was frozen solid, it was impossible to dig graves until spring. Something had to be done with the body until then. The answer for most farm families was the cooling board.

The body was wrapped in a cloth and strapped to a wide wooden plank and leaned up against an out-of-the-way corner of the barn or shed. The cold preserved the body until the ground thawed enough for burial. The process worked well enough in most cases, but there were exceptions.

I heard the following tale from a ninety-year-old man who now lives near Greeneville. He said that some mighty strange things happened to the recently departed before the days of undertakers, embalming, and the other niceties of modern funerals. I tell this story in pretty much the same words as he told it to me.

Pap caught a bad cold and died in January, right in the middle of the coldest snap Carter County had seen in thirty years. The ground was froze hard as a rock, so there was no chance we could bury him—not until spring anyway. Obviously something had to be done with Pap until then.

After the funeral, Daddy told me to go into the barn and find the big wide plank he was saving to fix one side of a watering trough that had almost rotted away. The plank was nearly two feet wide and about eight feet long—solid oak and nearly an inch thick.

"We'll use it to make a cooling board, strap Pap to it, and stand him up in a corner of the barn until the ground thaws enough to bury him," Daddy said. Then he added, "After Pap's finished with it, we'll use it to fix the trough."

I thought that was a mighty cruel way to treat kin—especially Pap. But my folks had done such things for years. Those were the days before we had backhoes to dig graves. When the ground was frozen solid, there was little you could do with a pick and shovel.

So I got the board and we strapped Pap to it. Then we set the plank up out in the barn in an out-of-the way corner. That was Mama's personal mandate. She said she didn't want to have to stare at Pap every time she went out to milk the cow.

It was my job to check up on the cooling board every day to make sure that no animals got to Pap's body. I didn't care much for the job, but it was only common decency that it be done.

One day in February, on the third day of an unusually warm spell, I went out to check on the body and Pap was gone—absolutely nowhere to be found. I asked Daddy if he had gone off and buried Pap without the rest of us knowing it. He said that he hadn't and ran into the barn to make sure I wasn't seeing things. Sure enough, the cooling board was there but Pap had vanished.

Daddy rounded up all the kids—there were six of us, counting me—and we fanned out into the surrounding woods looking for Pap. An hour later we were back empty-handed. Daddy was about to send us out again when, all of a sudden, the outhouse door opened and Pap ambled out.

"Howdy-do?" he chirped when he saw us there, our mouths standing open. "What's wrong?"

"What are you doing there, Daddy?" my father squeaked in astonishment. "You're supposed to be dead!"

"Reckon I ain't," Pap replied. "Leastwise, I don't think I am."

About that time, Mama came running out of the house and screamed loud enough to be heard clear to Nashville. She picked up her apron, turned on her heel, and ran back into the house, the screen door slamming behind her.

Pap scratched his head. "Now what do you s'pose is wrong with her?" he asked.

"I don't blame her a bit for acting like that," Daddy shouted excitedly. "You've been dead for almost a month! It was too cold to bury you, so we put you on a cooling board in the barn until the ground thawed. Now, suddenly, you're up and walking around."

Pap scratched his chin. "So that's why I woke up in the barn on that plank, all wrapped up and tied down like that."

"Yeah," Daddy answered. "That's why."

"And you say that I was froze solid for a month?"

"That's right."

"No wonder. I thought my joints were a mite stiffer than usual when I got up this morning."

It took the better part of two hours for Daddy to get Mama calmed down after she had seen Pap resurrected and walking around in the yard. That night the doctor—the same one who had pronounced Pap dead a month ago—came by to have a look.

After he had thoroughly examined him, the doctor declared that Pap was a modern medical miracle. "I've heard tell of things like this happening before, but I never thought I'd see it myself," he said as he packed his black bag and prepared to leave. "The old man must've had a spell and gone into a coma or something. At least, he fooled me. I thought he was really dead."

The doctor turned to Daddy and frowned. "When you put him on that cooling board and he froze solid, he was still alive. The cold kept him alive. Then when the temperature warmed up, he thawed out and woke up."

Pap smiled at the doctor. "I'm a tough old bird, ain't I, Doc?"

The doctor shook his finger in Pap's face. "Listen to me, you old coot," he shouted. "If your son, here, had had the money to have you embalmed proper, you would have stayed on that cooling board where you belonged. You can thank your lucky stars for poverty!"

Pap lived twenty more years after that. When he died again, it was at the ripe old age of ninety-eight. Since we didn't want to go through a second resurrection, we took Pap's body to an embalmer in Elizabethton and had the job done proper.

This time, Pap stayed where he belonged!

The Undertaker's Assistant

Sometimes a trickster gets more than he bargained for, and sometimes an innocent trick can turn tragic, like in this hair-raising tale from Upper East Tennessee.

One night many years ago, toward the end of a four-day drenching rain, a local Sullivan County farmer was awakened by the ringing of his telephone. When he answered he found himself talking to a local undertaker who, by the sound of his voice, was obviously in great distress.

"Mr. Simms, I've got a hearse stuck down in Reedy Creek. I went over to Bristol to take a dead man, and now I can't get the hearse out of the creek. My old horse ain't as strong as your mule. I hate to bother you on a night like this, but could you give me some help?"

"Sure," Mr. Simms answered. "I'll get the mule and I think I can get you out all right. But I'm going to need your help."

"Mr. Simms, I can't get out there. After I unhitched the horse and rode him back to the office, there were two more bodies to pick up. So I have to hitch up my spare hearse right away and go out to get them. I'm sorry."

"It's been raining mighty hard, and I understand that creek's in mighty bad condition. But I still think I may need more help than just my mule."

"All right, sir. I got a man down here at the office. He was going to help me, but I can spare him. I'll send him right

over to where I'm mired in. He'll meet you there. And thank you for your kindness."

The undertaker's office was located a pretty good distance from the hearse stuck in the creek. The farmer figured that by the time he led his mule out of the barn and rode him to the location, the undertaker's man still would not have had a chance to get there. He also knew that the assistant—if it was the same one he was thinking of—was highly superstitious. The opportunity that presented itself was simply too good to be true. He could have himself a little fun—some payment, at least, for being dragged out on a night such as this.

With this in mind he searched around his barn until he found a long length of strong twine. Then he bridled his mule, slid onto his back, and rode off into the night.

The hearse was about five miles from the undertaker's office and a two-mile ride for the farmer. The rain had slacked off a bit, but it was still coming down pretty hard. The black horse-drawn hearse was in the swollen creek all right, covered with muddy water past the axles. Through the glass on the side Mr. Simms could see the body lying peacefully inside.

All the kerosene lanterns were still burning on the hearse, and their yellow light cast an eerie glow in the surrounding woods. Mr. Simms looked around just to make sure that the undertaker's man had not yet appeared. No, he was alone in the woods. Mr. Simms dismounted and, with the twine in his hand and a smirk on his face, waded through the coffee-colored water to the hearse.

He opened the back door of the wagon. The body, of course, was wrapped in a shroud. Mr. Simms tied one end of the twine to the body, then closed the door. With his mule's tether in one hand and the twine in the other, Mr. Simms waded the rest of the way across rain-swollen Reedy Creek. Then he hid the mule and hunkered down behind a nearby tree to await the undertaker's assistant.

A half hour later Mr. Simms spied a lantern shining in the woods, swinging to and fro, approaching the hearse. Then came a youthful voice calling out, "Mr. Simms? You here yet?"

Of course, Mr. Simms said nothing. He peered into the darkness and recognized the figure of a young boy of about seventeen—the undertaker's helper whose name was John. He was a tall, gangly lad who had worked for the undertaker for about six months. Mr. Simms could see from the expression on the lad's face that he was not happy about being alone in the woods—especially with a hearse and a dead body.

The boy held the lantern up so that he could see the hearse better. Then he looked around nervously, obviously hoping that help would soon arrive. He slowly waded out into swollen Reedy Creek and approached the rear door of the hearse. Since it was so dark, he didn't notice the twine hanging from a crack at the bottom of the door. In the meantime, Mr. Simms poised himself behind a the tree, his hand firmly grasping the twine.

Reaching for the latch, the lad opened the rear door just a crack as if gathering up the courage to open it all the way. This was the first time he had been alone with a dead body, and he was plainly nervous.

Finally he opened the door and peered into the hearse. The body was there, all right—wrapped tightly in its linen shroud. Suddenly Mr. Simms jerked the twine and pulled the body into a sitting position. Then he shouted in a deep, hoarse voice, "This is Mike. This is Mike. I done come back to life. I done come back to life. Let me out."

The startled boy yelled, and his scream echoed through the trees. He dropped his lantern and slammed the hearse door so hard that the twine was cut in two. The body fell back into a prone position with a thump. The sudden slack in the twine caused Mr. Simms to lose his balance, and he fell back into a clump of wet leaves. By the time he regained his feet, the boy was nowhere to be seen.

I bet he's gonna run all the way back to the undertaker, Mr. Simms chuckled to himself as he waded back across the creek, leading the mule.

It was no trouble at all for Mr. Simms to hook up the mule to the hearse and pull the vehicle out of the stream. Then Mr. Simms snapped the reins and headed toward town. About a mile down the road, he saw a figure in front of him. It was the undertaker's assistant, totally drenched from head to foot, also heading for town.

Mr. Simms and the hearse drew up alongside the lad, who stopped and looked up. "Wanna ride?" Mr. Simms asked the boy.

"That was a dirty trick you played on me, Mr. Simms," the boy said.

Mr. Simms laughed. "If that's the worst thing that ever happens to you, boy, count yourself lucky. Now, do you want a ride or not?"

"Yes, sir," the boy replied as he climbed up into the boot of the hearse and settled in beside the driver. Then Mr. Simms snapped the reins once again and not another word was exchanged between them.

When they arrived outside the undertaker's office, the boy jumped from the hearse. "I'll go in and get the boss," he told Mr. Simms.

"All right, boy," Mr. Simms replied, and the boy stepped up on the porch.

Five minutes passed. *Where is that boy?* Mr. Simms asked himself. Several minutes later he decided to go into the office himself and find out what was holding things up.

Inside he found the undertaker sitting at his desk, doing some paperwork. "What are you doing here?" Mr. Simms asked. "Here I'm standing outside with your hearse, getting wetter by the second, and you're working at your desk. Didn't your assistant tell you that I was outside?"

The undertaker looked up from his work. There was a surprised look on his face. "I'm sorry," he said. "I didn't know you were out there."

"Didn't that boy tell you where I was? He came in here ten minutes ago."

"Mr. Simms, the only one who's been in this office all evening is me!"

The next day, the sheriff and his deputies found the waterlogged body of the undertaker's assistant in the swollen waters of Reedy Creek. After Mr. Simms told them about the joke that he had pulled on the young fellow, the only thing they could figure was that he had lost his footing in the fast-moving water and had been swept away with the stream. For years after, the ghost of the drowned undertaker's assistant was seen often walking through the woods.

Of course, Mr. Simms was guilt-ridden for the rest of his days over the incident. In fact, in the last years of his life, he became a recluse—hardly ever leaving his farm, even to go into town for supplies. And it is said that he was never able to completely shake the ghost of the undertaker's assistant until the day he died. Because on each rainy night he would hear a knock on the door, and when he answered it, he would find the apparition of the drenched lad standing before him.

On the cold and rainy night that Mr. Simms died he was sitting by the fire with one of his few friends. As they sat warming their innards with a bottle of whiskey that the friend had brought with him, there was a knock at the door.

"It's him again," Mr. Simms said in a whisper. "He comes

at least once on every night like this. I open the door and he stands there. I shut the door and open it again, and he's gone. It's happened so many times that I'm not even scared anymore."

Mr. Simms stood up. "Pardon me for a second while I open the door and get rid of our friend. It will only take a second."

The nervous friend, of course, had no desire to see a ghost so he turned his head and poured a stiff drink. Mr. Simms walked over to the door and opened it.

Suddenly a horrible scream filled the farmhouse. When the startled friend turned toward the door, Mr. Simms had vanished. The door was standing open while wind-lashed rain blew through the opening.

The next day, Mr. Simms's waterlogged body was found in the overflowing waters of Reedy Creek. On his face was a frozen expression of horror. And the ghost of the undertaker's assistant was never seen again.

NOTE: *When a friend of mine, Russell Tharp of Egg Harbor Township, New Jersey, read this story, he offered a similar tale of a prank gone wrong. This one, too, had tragic consequences:*

The following is a tale my great-grandfather used to tell. Seems that many years ago it was the custom to lay out the bodies of the recently dead in their parlors before the burial, and to have a friend or relative sit up with them for the night. Well, one day old man Johnson finally passed, and some of the town's men saw the chance to play a great joke on Johnson's grandson, Peter.

Peter was big, mean, and quite slow witted. He was disliked by nearly everyone in town. Yet this oaf stood to inherit all of old man Johnson's not-insubstantial cash and property. The boy should be made to pay a bit for all that windfall, they thought, and they quickly developed a plan.

As the sole heir to Johnson's estate, the duty to sit up with the body would fall to Peter. Peter was known to be a superstitious sort, and the men decided to give him the scare of his life. A few of the men drew Peter from the parlor to old man

Johnson's den, on the excuse of toasting the dead man with some fine scotch whiskey. While Peter was thus distracted, the other men stole away with Johnson's shrouded body, and another man, also wrapped in linen, took his place. The men made their excuses to depart and left, sneaking around to a side window to watch the fun. As planned, a few minutes later, at the stroke of midnight, the man under the sheet moaned and slowly sat up.

Peter was horrified, but not in the way the men had expected. "Oh, no you don't!" he cried. "That money was mine when I came in here, and it's gonna be mine when I leave!" Peter then proceeded to take a poker from the fireplace and bludgeon the jokester in the sheet to death.

It's not a happy story....

The Vision

Some folks, it is said, receive visions but never act on them because they are considered mere dreams. In his 1911 book, From Log Cabin to the Pulpit, or, Fifteen Years in Slavery, *the Rev. W. H. Robinson tells of one woman who followed her dream, however, and received an unexpected reward. Here is my edited version of Pastor Robinson's story.*

In 1864, near Blue Springs, Tennessee, three union soldiers became separated from their army. When passing through a small oak grove, one of them got into the quicksand. The others, supposing their companion was closely following them, pursued their course.

This poor hero was left behind, struggling for his life in the quicksand for three days and nights, buoying himself up from sinking with the aid of such sticks and brush as he could reach.

This location was but a short distance from a large southern mansion. The men had all gone to war, and there were left but a few old colored mothers to protect the old mistress.

Aunt Nancy Jordan dreamed one night—or saw a vision as she termed it—that she saw a man in trouble near the springs and that she heard a voice saying, "Nancy, go to the east spring." She claimed to have heard that call three different times that night in her dreams, and early the next morning she took her pail and went to the spring.

When near the place, she heard a human voice pleading for help. She then realized her dream, or presentiment, and on looking saw a Union soldier buried to his armpits in the quicksand. She knew just what it meant and started toward him. He murmured for her not to come too close.

Her reply was, "God bless you, child. I know all about this place."

She felt her way as close to him as possible until she felt the quicksand giving way under her. Then she gathered brush and bridged her way over to him, near enough to reach him with a long-handled gourd.

She then went to the spring, which was not over twenty feet away, and secured water for him, as his tongue was so badly swollen that he could scarcely speak. She held the gourd to his lips, slaked his thirst, and then began the work of rescue, piling brush around him. She got hold of his arms and assisted him out so that he could sit upon the brush.

That spring was never used by the people from the mansion on account of the quicksand and alkali in the water. Nancy returned to the house with her pail of water, then hurried back with food in the pail upon her head. In this way she fed him for three weeks, at the end of which time one morning she heard the tramp, tramp of a mighty army.

Bands were playing and bugles sounding. Then she saw old Missie scampering for the cellar, for, said she, "Nancy, they are Lincoln's hirelings, for they are all dressed in blue."

Aunt Nancy hurried to the spring and told the soldier that the Yankees were coming. He at once came from his hiding place. When he reached the yard of that mansion, he found it swarming with Union soldiers. He said to Aunt Nancy, "I can't leave you here, for you must go with us."

She replied, "I promised old master not to leave old Missie till he comes back from the war." But he assured her that it meant her freedom, and asked if she had not prayed to be free? She replied, "Yes, sir," and that if it meant her freedom she would bid old Missie good-bye.

There was a pathetic scene at this parting. Old mistress ventured to the porch and took her last long look at her old ex-slave as the Yankee soldier was helping her into the wagon.

Aunt Nancy became cook in the camp for the officers, and this soldier, whom she had rescued, looked after her as though she were his mother. He was an Englishman and had come to this country about the time of the beginning of the war. He naturalized and enlisted.

When he was discharged he took Aunt Nancy to England with him and presented her to his mother as the preserver of his life. She had been in London two years or more when I arrived there, and was among the most honored women of the city.

She came back to America on the same steamer that I came on. She was certainly looked upon as a sanctified Christian woman.

The soldier who took her over was bringing her back. He would have her dress in the same costume she wore when she rescued him from the quicksand, and thus gave an exhibition every few days. She was not now the same illiterate Aunt Nancy that she was three years ago, for contact with educated and refined people had polished her up wonderfully.

The Coffin That Wouldn't Stay Buried

Here's a tale from the Northwest corner of Tennessee about greed and a very mobile coffin. It fact, this story might not even be a ghost tale at all. You be the judge.

One cold night, many years ago, the meanest man in town died a horrible death. Folks say that he was sitting inside his bank vault counting his money when the heavy steel door closed by accident, trapping him inside with all his wealth. When his assistant opened the vault door the next morning, they found the old miser sprawled on the floor—asphyxiated—still grasping loose coins in his hand.

Of course the town was unmoved at his passing. The old man hated everyone and everything. He was also very rich and owned the only town bank. That meant that most people in the neighborhood were indebted to him one way or the other. But they would take out a loan only as a last resort. They knew that he always went by the letter of his loan agreements and would never grant an extension, even for those in dire need.

Over the years dozens of honest home owners' and farmers' properties were repossessed because of the old man's greed. So, naturally, no tears were shed when his miserable life finally ended. "Good riddance," most said. "Serves him right!" No one, in fact, even attended his funeral, except the preacher (who was getting paid to conduct the service) and the old man's son.

The boy, unlike his father, however, was good and kind. Since he was the old man's legal heir, he inherited the family money and the bank as well. The old man and the boy never did get along very well. The father detested his son's generosity and the son detested his father's stinginess.

"You can't take it with you," the son would tell his father.

"Oh, yeah?" the old man would always growl back. "Watch me."

With the old man finally dead, a collective sigh of relief arose in the community. With his son in his place there was hope that those in debt might have a fighting chance to keep their heads above water and not lose everything they owned.

Soon after the old man was buried in his sleek black coffin in the church graveyard, strange things began to happen. The coffin would not stay buried.

Each evening the town grave digger would rebury the coffin, only to have it reappear—halfway in the ground and halfway out of the ground. The town was thoroughly spooked, and the talk was that the old miser was trying to crawl out of his coffin to get back to his gold.

"Nonsense," the miser's son said. "This ground is honeycombed with caves. Something under there is causing that coffin to come to the surface."

"That may be true," one of the townsmen said, "but what about the other graves? Why are they not affected?"

The boy had no answer for that one. But, at the same time, he said that he could not accept the notion of a dead man trying to get out of a coffin, especially to retrieve gold that he had no use for whatsoever.

"I think that I will go down to the churchyard tonight and see what is happening for myself," he said. "Anyone want to go along?"

"Not me," the townspeople said.

"Very well," the boy replied. "Then I will go myself!"

When the young man failed to show up for work the next morning, the head teller and his assistant assumed that he was ill. But when they opened the bank vault, they discovered to their horror that all the money was gone. Instead they found small piles of foul smelling moldy earth scattered all over the floor.

The sheriff was contacted, and a small group of men went to the house of the miser's son to look for him. He was not there. Then someone remembered that the young man said that he was going out to the graveyard to investigate the matter of the coffin that wouldn't stay buried.

When they got there the young man was nowhere to be seen. Furthermore, the old man's coffin, which apparently had worked itself to the surface every night since the burial, was nowhere in sight either. In fact, for the first time, the grave appeared not to have been disturbed.

Through the years the mystery has remained. Where was all the money that had been in the vault? It was never found. And where was the son of the old miser? He was never found either. Was he, in fact, a con man who had taken the money and skipped town? Or had something else—something unspeakable—happened to him?

There is, of course, the persistent legend that the old man really did come back from the dead and take all his money into the coffin with him. And it is said that somewhere in that old churchyard thousands upon thousands of dollars are still scattered among the dry bones of an old miser, and maybe even his son.

The problem is, however, no one—so far, at least—has had the courage to try to dig it up!

The Light in the Forest

Here is a story from Robertson County, home of the infamous Bell Witch of Tennessee. However, this tale is not about the Witch.

In Robertson County, forty miles north of Nashville, just off of State Route 431, there is a small patch of woods that is said to house a mysterious ghost light. In the woods, at that point, is an Indian burial mound, and it is naturally assumed that the light is actually the ghost of a restless warrior who refuses to stay buried.

On very dark nights this light rises up from the thick underbrush, floats through the trees, and eventually emerges into an open field. The light has been described as having a pale yellow glow about the size of a basketball. As it travels on its way, it sizzles and pops like a live electric wire. Sometimes the faint form of a head is seen inside the globe.

The strange object is well-known in the neighborhood, and the little woods is a popular spot with the young and adventurous. Of course, people try to catch the light, and the object seems to have a sense of humor, because it likes to play "keep-away" with its pursuers. It darts in and out of the trees. It stands still while someone approaches. Just as the pursuer is about to grab it, the light darts out of the way. No one has ever caught it.

One day, however, the light became more than just a

ghostly plaything. It became the neighborhood hero.

A little girl wandered away from home and got lost in the rugged hill country of Robertson County. She had been missing several hours, and her father had searched everywhere for her. Then he called the sheriff. The sheriff, in turn, called out his deputies. They feared the worst. It was very cold and blustery that day, the temperature well below freezing. A small child could not last long out in this kind of weather.

It was getting late, and darkness promised to lower the temperature even more. Deputies and neighbors fanned out over the hills and fields of Robertson County, desperately calling the little girl's name. There was no reply.

Finally the search neared the little patch of woods where the ghost light lurked. It was almost dark now, but an eerie light shown through the trees. The men looked over toward the woods and, yes, there it was. The ghost light hung about four feet off the ground, glowing brightly. But this time it looked different. Instead of a steady glow, this time the light was pulsating, as if trying to get someone's attention.

Several of the men broke from the group and began walking toward the light. The sheriff called out to them.

"Come on, fellas," he shouted. "We don't have the time to chase that thing."

"But it's not moving like it usually does," one of the men called back. "Look!"

He was right. The light stood as still as a stone as the men approached it. Then another man shouted, "Here she is! Under the light!"

The rest of the searchers came running. Sure enough, there was the little girl, none the worse for wear, lying on a bed of leaves, fast asleep.

The ghost light slowly rose until it was about fifteen feet over the head of the rescuers. Then it slowly started to fade. When the little girl awoke, she asked the whereabouts of the nice man.

"What nice man?" the relieved father asked as he cradled the little girl in his arms.

"I was lost," she said. "And this nice man came to me and led me here. He fixed some leaves so that I could have a soft bed to lie on. Then he told me to go to sleep and that he would watch over me."

The father frowned. "What did the man look like, honey?"

"An Indian."

The men looked up above their heads as the last shimmer of the ghost light disappeared into the night. The spirit of the Indian had found the little lost girl and had protected her until help could arrive.

The child's father wondered how he could possibly thank a ghost for saving his daughter. The next time he saw the ghost light, he could try to make contact with it and show how grateful he was.

But he never got that chance. The ghost light was never seen again.

A Haunted Path

The Indian was probably the first environmentalist in America. Everything he did was, in one way or another, tied to the land. Even his religion was nature-based. He had his spirits of the water, spirits of the forest, and spirits of the mountains—and great respect for all of it. White settlers, on the other hand, cut trees, dammed streams, and farmed the land until all the nutrients were drained away. Finally, when the land gave out, they moved farther west to greener pastures.

The effect was horrendous. During the Great Depression, for instance, a series of devastating floods inundated the Tennessee Valley. One of the major causes was overcutting of lumber farther west in the watersheds of the Missouri River, Mississippi River, etc. With the foliage gone, there was nothing to hold rainwater, which poured into streams.

The creation of the Tennessee Valley Authority and the building of hydroelectric dams in the Tennessee Valley helps prevent much of this flooding today. Trees in the watersheds have returned. We are lucky in that respect. It was not too late to right a terrible wrong.

In the past fifty years, Americans have become more conscious of the preservation of forest land. Today there seems to be more forest in America than there was in Colonial times, but little of it is virgin timber. Most is second or third growth which, in many instances, is scraggly. There are, however, a few pockets of this virgin forest left. The U.S. government tries

to preserve this land as best it can, but there is still encroach-
ment. Lumber, paper, and building interests constantly put
pressure on lawmakers to allow verdant forest to be used for
commercial interests.

One great patch of virgin forest still exists on the Ten-
nessee/North Carolina border. In the Great Smoky Mountains
National Park the total amount of undisturbed land exceeds
that of any other deciduous and coniferous forest in the United
States south of New York state's Adirondack Park.

During the time of the great removal, when the government
was forcing the Cherokee onto the reservation in Oklahoma,
many Native Americans fled to the Smokies to escape federal
authorities attempting to round them up. The mountains were
their homeland, and they were determined to fight relocation
to Indian Territory. Some of the fugitives were never rooted out.
It was claimed that the forest spirits protected and hid them.
Some of those spirits are said to still exist—to still protect the
forest, should the Cherokee return to their homeland and once
again take up the old ways.

On one of the main hiking trails, through one of the best
stands of pristine virgin growth, there is even said to be a
haunted path.

The story is that a section of the Great Smoky Mountains is guarded by a powerful Cherokee spirit that protects the land from harm. A number of people claim to have seen it— a face enveloped in smoke or mist, hovering just above the path, gazing sternly at intruders who would do the forest harm.

A Cherokee legend tells of a medicine man, finally forced to join his fellow tribesmen on the infamous "Trail of Tears," who left the spirit in place to protect his homeland just in case he was someday allowed to return. Whether or not he was allowed to return, or whether he died on the trek to Indian Territory—over 4,000 Cherokee did—is unknown. But the protecting spirit, by all reports, is still firmly in place.

Many is the startled soul who has been suddenly con- fronted by the spirit of the haunted path. A well-known encounter involved a family who, several years ago, decided to backpack through some of the more remote areas of the Great Smoky Mountains. This family—a mother and father and their two sons—had been on the trail for almost two days. On the third, they decided to camp for the night in a little glade just off the haunted path.

The entire family was thoroughly experienced with life in the woods. From the time they could understand, the boys had been taught to respect nature, to be careful with fire, and to leave a campsite unmarked by their passing. Yet the boys, aged eight and ten, were still boys and not immune to abusing nature in the spirit of fun. In fact, the oldest had a cruel streak toward animals that worried his parents considerably. He had once tried to throw a large firecracker next to a sleeping cat in order to see it jump. Unfortunately, the boy's aim was off and the firecracker landed directly on the cat's back. It exploded and severely injured the animal. The boy was grounded for a week after the incident, and the cat, obviously, was never the same again.

That night the family made camp and settled down to their evening meal. Afterward, they sat around the campfire and told ghost stories. The eight-year-old was an impressionable lad and quite shaken by one of the stories in particular that his father told—the tale of the haunted path.

"Is that the path there," he asked his father, pointing, "the one we just came up on?"

"I can't say," the father replied. "It could be. There are many paths running through this forest. Most have never been mapped. But we have nothing to fear from the spirit. We are not hurting the forest. The spirit only appears when someone is destroying something—maybe cutting a tree. We haven't done that. Our firewood was already lying on the ground when we gathered it."

But the young fellow was not entirely convinced that the spirit would not appear. For the rest of the night, before the family crawled into their sleeping bags for the night, the boy would glance nervously toward the trail in the woods. The older boy could not help but notice his brother's uneasiness, and he decided to take advantage of the situation.

The family had brought two tents on the outing—one for the parents and one for the boys. After dark the boys were curled up inside their tent, quietly listening to the sounds of the night. Finally the older boy said to his brother, "Did you believe what Dad said about that Indian spirit out there on the trail?"

"I don't even want to talk about it," the younger boy said, still very nervous at the thought of a ghost lurking nearby.

"I'd like to see it," the older brother continued.

"I said, I don't want to talk about it," the younger one repeated.

Without another word, the older boy crawled out of his sleeping bag.

"Where you going?" the younger one asked.

"Shhhh.... Quiet. You'll wake up Mom and Dad."

"I-I said, where are you going?"

The older brother paused at the tent fly. "I'm going out to try to see the spirit."

"You'll get into trouble."

"I've been in trouble before."

"I'll say you have. But I'd stay in here if I were you. You go out there you might get eat up by a bear, or worse."

"Chicken heart!" the older boy chided his brother.

"I'm still not coming!"

"Suit yourself," the older boy said as he unzipped the tent fly. "But you're gonna miss out on all the fun!"

"Oh, no I'm not," the younger brother said as he scrambled out of his sleeping bag. "I'm right behind you."

It seemed as if the woods were considerably darker than when the boys went to bed. They quietly tiptoed out of camp so as not to wake their parents. A minute later they were standing on the trail that led through the woods.

"So?" the young fellow asked. "What do we do now?"

"We're going to see if we can summon up the spirit that's supposed to be out here, of course."

"And just how are you going to do that? You just can't say, 'Spirit, show yourself.'"

The older brother got a real disgusted look on his face. "Don't you think that I know that? Now, let's see. What did Dad say would make the spirit appear?"

"Didn't he say that the spirit was here to protect the woods and if you did something bad to the trees then the spirit would show up?"

"Uh, huh."

"So what are you going to do?"

The older brother reached into his belt and pulled out a big trail knife. "I'm going to do a little hacking on some trees."

Just as he was about to start whacking away at a little birch, the boys heard a sudden noise off to their right. Both jumped like scalded cats.

There it was again! The sound! Flop. Rustle. Flop. Rustle. Flop. Rustle.

It was coming from the ground at their feet. The older boy looked down. Then he grinned. "It ain't nothing but a big old hoppy toad," he said. "I'll fix him...."

"No! Don't...," the younger brother shouted out. But it was too late. The older boy had already hurled the knife, which struck its mark, impaling the toad.

"That'll teach you to scare me!" the boy said laughing.

"You killed it," his young brother cried. "Why did you have to go and kill it? It wasn't hurting you!"

"Awww, it was just an old toad," the older boy said. "Ain't no account. There's plenty more where that came from." He reached over to retrieve his knife, but the toad wasn't there. He searched the immediate area of the knife. The mark the sharp point had made was on the path, but the dead toad was nowhere to be found.

"Oh, well," he said, "I'm getting tired of this. We're not going to see anything. Let's go back to bed."

No sooner had the boys turned around to return to the campsite than they saw a faint glow among the trees. Must be the moon coming out, they thought. But the light grew brighter and brighter. Then the boys saw a luminescent ball of mist floating up the trail, coming steadily toward them. They stood frozen in their tracks.

When the ball got to within fifty feet of where they were standing, they could see an indistinct face hovering in the center of the swirling cloud. The face was old—ancient. A huge hook nose, like one would see on a very old man, was poised above a wrinkled mouth that almost looked like it was smiling at them. And above that were two huge bulbous eyes  that seemed to glow from a source of yellow light located somewhere inside the head.

The apparition stared at the two terrified boys for a moment. Then it said in a horse whisper, "Where is brother toad?"

The boys, at the moment, could not muster the courage to speak.

The apparition asked again, "I said, where is brother toad?"

Again, words were stuck in each boy's throat.

"Did you kill him?" the apparition asked. Then it stared directly at the oldest brother. "Why did you slay brother toad?"

"S-sir?" the oldest boy finally stammered.

"He was the oldest and largest in the forest," the apparition told them. "His friends were many and his enemies were few." The apparition continued staring.

"I-I think we'd better get back to camp now," the younger brother said.

"No, young buck," the apparition said. "I have something for you."

"M-me?"

The apparition smiled. "It was you who tried to prevent your brother from throwing the knife. You are kind, and for this you shall be rewarded. No more will your brother cause you to be taken in by his evil tricks. I give you the gift of wisdom. Use it well."

"Now just one doggoned minute here...," the older boy began.

Suddenly the boys heard a loud croak. They looked toward the ground and saw the toad sitting at their feet, very much alive. Then it turned and followed the receding spirit into the depths of the woods.

The older boy looked at his little brother in utter amazement. He started to speak, but he could see right away there was something different about the little boy—a look in his eyes.

From that day on, the older one could never put one over on the young boy again. The little kid was just too darned smart to be taken in.

The Phantom Rooster

The rooster's distinctive call is almost always associated with rural life. The cock-a-doodle-doo *heralds morning and is considered nature's alarm clock. But take that same familiar sound and attach it to the unknown and you have the stuff of which goose bumps are made. Take, for example, this improbable tale.*

The story of the phantom rooster began almost one hundred years ago when a farmer named Blane lost his entire flock of chickens to a mysterious disease. It was said that he had offended a woman who was a witch, and she had cursed his hens and had predicted that all of them would die. The only bird left out of the flock was an old rooster that Blane had named Bernard.

Bernard was Blane's pet. The old bird had been living in the barnyard for years and followed Blane around like a faithful dog. Blane would save the best feed for Bernard and often fed him by hand. Even on cold winter nights, Blane would invite Bernard into the house so that he would not have to endure the cold. In return, Bernard did a good job fertilizing eggs, and Blane was the proud owner of one of the best flocks of chickens in the county. That, of course, all changed when his flock died.

Now Blane had a problem on his hands. What should he do with Bernard? He was no more use since the hens were all gone. But, on the other hand, the place would not seem the same without Bernard to wake Blane up in the morning. Besides, Bernard was a pet.

With all the chickens gone, however, Blane was starting to get hungry. He had had no other livestock on his farm except the chickens. He had eaten their eggs morning, noon, and night. But out of respect to Bernard, Blane had refrained from eating the chickens.

Blane also owned a sawmill, located on his farm. But business was down, there, too. In fact, Blane had not sawed a board in over two months. As his stomach became increasingly empty, the rooster began to look better and better as a tasty dinner.

Finally, one day, Blane went out to the woodshed and got his sharpest axe. Then he walked out into the barnyard and began looking for Bernard. He found the rooster pecking around the yard, looking for a nice, big, juicy worm to eat. He tried to sneak up behind the bird, but Bernard saw him coming. One look at the axe in Blane's hand was enough to send the rooster scurrying for cover, with Blane in hot pursuit. Just as Blane was about to catch up to him, Bernard ducked under a woodpile.

"Come out of there, rooster," Blane shouted into the darkness. Of course, Bernard didn't answer, but Blane could hear the rustling of his feathers beneath the woodpile. "I said," Blane repeated, "COME OUT OF THERE!!!!"

Blane leaned his axe against the woodpile and began to remove the logs one by one. He didn't think that it would take him very long to uncover the hiding rooster, but by nightfall, he was not even half finished.

"You might as well come out of there now," Blane said. "I'm gonna get you sooner or later."

By now, Blane's stomach was growling like an old she-bear with cubs. If he didn't get that rooster out of the woodpile pretty soon, he would starve to death. He worked quickly to remove the rest of the logs before it got much darker. He didn't want to take the chance that Bernard would escape.

Finally he was almost to the bottom. He should be able to

see the rooster pretty soon. Suddenly there was a fluttering of wings, and Bernard flew out of the woodpile, nearly knocking Blane over in the process. Before Blane could grab his axe, Bernard was halfway across the barnyard and winging toward the sawmill. In his desperate flight, the rooster wasn't looking where he was going and he ran right into the saw. The sharp blade caught him in the neck and severed his head from his body. By the time Blane got there, Bernard's head was lying on one side and his body was flopping around on the other.

That night, Blane had fried chicken for dinner. Then, later that night, the rooster came back.

About ten p.m., filled to the brim with chicken, Blane went to bed. He had just fallen asleep when he was startled awake by the crowing of a rooster. He jumped out of bed and ran to the window. Peering out into the misty darkness he thought he saw a rooster perched on the barnyard fence. In fact, he thought that he recognized the rooster as his own Bernard.

Impossible, he thought to himself. *Bernard was eaten for supper. It couldn't be him. It must be someone else's rooster.*

The rooster crowed again.

Blane knew he was not going to get any sleep as long as that noisy bird was sitting on his fence, so he decided that he would go down into the barnyard and shoo him away. He slipped on his pants and shoes, then walked downstairs and out the door.

There was a slight chill to the night air, and Blane wished that he had pulled on a shirt. *Oh, well*, he thought. *I might as well get this over with so I can crawl back into my nice warm bed.*

Blane walked across the barnyard. The rooster was still perched on the fence post, his feathery shape outlined by the moonlight. "Get out of here, rooster," Blane shouted. "I have to get my sleep."

The rooster turned and looked at the figure approaching him. Then he reared back his head and crowed so loudly that it hurt Blane's ears. Then the rooster turned again to the man and said, "Is that loud enough or would you like me to crow a little louder?"

Blane stopped and stared in disbelief. A talking rooster? The bird raised his foot to his head as if to scratch. Instead, he grabbed his own head in his claws and lifted it off his shoulders. He tipped it toward Blane like a man tipping his hat. Then the rooster replaced the head on his shoulders where it belonged.

"Now, that's better. Do you recognize me, Blane?"

"Bernard?"

"Yeah. Me."

"But you're dead."

"Right again. In fact, I'm so dead that you're looking at my ghost. Now how do you like that?"

Blane did not like it. Not one little bit.

"Furthermore," the rooster added, "I have another surprise for you. Since I got eaten by you, I can crow louder than before. And, by jimminy, that's exactly what I'm going to do."

And crow he did—so loud, in fact, that Blane had to hold his ears. When Bernard stopped his crowing, Blane lowered his arms. "Listen," he told the rooster, "I was hungry. I'm sorry if I...."

"But you did eat me," Bernard interrupted. "That makes all the difference. All those years we were friends. Then the minute your stomach starts rumbling a little bit, you have to go and introduce me to the frying pan. Such gratitude. Now I'm going to get my revenge for your greed. I'm going to crow and crow and never let you sleep again."

"Now let's not be too hasty, Bernard," Blane said. "Surely we can work something out."

"With me still inside you?" Bernard asked. "You have your nerve even suggesting something like that."

"But if I don't get any sleep, I'll die!" Blane whined.

Bernard smiled. But instead of answering his former friend he reared back his head and let go with one of the most ear shattering cock-a-doodle-doos ever heard. Blane knew that there was no reasoning with the rooster, so he began to think of ways that he could outsmart him.

"COCK-A-DOODLE-DOO!!!!!"

Blane's hands shot up to his ears. His eardrums burned with the screeching sound.

"COCK-A-DOODLE-DOO!!!!!"

Suddenly Blane had an idea. He lunged at the rooster and grabbed hold of the bird's ghostly head, which, of course, came off quite easily in his hand.

"COCK-A-DOODLE-DOO!!!!!"

Blane ran over to a very deep, long-dried-up well and threw the rooster's head into the black pit. All the way to the bottom the rooster's head sang.

"COCK-A-DOODLE-DOO!!!!!"

Blane ran to the barn and grabbed a shovel and began hurling dirt into the well. He worked all night and most of the next day filling up that well. By the time that he had finished he was exhausted. He sat down beside the well and leaned up against the stone wall that circled the now-filled-in hole. When he looked up he saw the ghost of the headless rooster standing in front of him, gesturing wildly with his wings.

"You can complain all you want to," Blane said. "I am not going to dig up your head. Without a mouth you can make no noise and I will be able to get some sleep. You're just going to have to get over it."

So for the rest of his life Blane was haunted by the ghost of the rooster. Whenever he went to town, the ghost followed him. In fact, he became quite an item of gossip when the townsfolk saw him doing his errands closely shadowed by a ghostly rooster without a head. Finally, after a long time, the gossip died down and the ghost was accepted as the norm.

As for Blane, he would have liked it much better without the constant presence of the ghost of the headless rooster. But he figured it was a small price to pay for his mistake of eating Bernard for dinner. At least, since the head was now at the bottom of a fifty-foot, filled-in well, the shrieking call of the bird was heard no more and he could get some sleep.

That was at least peace for him—of sorts.

NOTE: *Another story about a beheaded rooster comes from—of all places—New York City. James McGinness told this tale to WPA worker and fellow New Yorker A. Fitzpatrick in 1938:*

A brother-in-law of mine, living on East 225th Street in the upper Bronx, occupied a little five-room, one-family house. In the rear he had a garden where he grew, each year, a plentiful supply of vegetables. He was a great lover of flowers, too, and at one time had as much as thirty-one different varieties in bloom at the same time.

At the rear of the garden he had erected a six-by-four chicken coop and a forty-foot-long runway for the chickens to exercise in. He had forty chickens, including a magnificent specimen of a rooster, standing nearly two feet in height. And how that boy could crow.

This brother-in-law of mine, that I'm speaking about, was a taxicab driver. He arose every morning at four a.m. and left the house at five to be at his work at six. He retired to bed every night at nine p.m. The only trouble was that he could not secure a night's unbroken sleep due to the crowing of the rooster.

He confided in his wife, adding, "That rooster's got to go." A few days afterward, upon his return from a hard day's work, he took the axe, grabbed the rooster, took him to the chopping block, and severed his head from his body! The rooster ran around, headless, for a while and then collapsed. Chicken fricassee didn't taste bad that evening for supper.

The next night, the one following the demise of the rooster, my brother-in-law was awakened in the early hours. He was not sure, so he listened again. There it was. The rooster was still crowing. There was no mistake about it. He knew that he was not dreaming, because the crowing was repeated while he lay in his bed.

Not wishing to alarm his wife, he told her nothing about his experience of the night. He went to sleep again the next night and, sure enough, the rooster woke him up again. He wanted to tell his wife but, knowing how Irish and superstitious she was, he kept his knowledge to himself.

However, the third night was too much for him. He was beginning to get nervous. All he knew, and was sure of, was THAT HE HAD KILLED THAT DARNED ROOSTER—and being over twenty-one he had sense enough to know that dead roosters CAN'T crow. He had only one rooster at the time; he had none now; so where was the crowing coming from?

He hit upon a plan. He got up and dressed and, taking a flashlight and an axe with him, went out into the night and down to the chicken coop. He placed his hand on the wire mesh enclosing the runway and waited. He wasn't disappointed. Sure enough, there it was, and right inside the coop— "Cock-a-doodle-do." He almost dropped the axe when his hair stood on end, but gathering his courage (or what was left of it), he rushed to the coop, tore open the door and looked in. There were the chickens all asleep, huddled up close to each other and—no ROOSTER. He closed the door quickly and bolted for the house. When he was safely inside, he woke his wife up and told her the story.

His wife looked at him to see if he had been drinking and said, "Are ye losin' ye're senses? Ye know that ye killed that rooster three days ago and that we ate him. Now hold ye're whisht and get back into bed. Waking a body up with such a fool tale as that. G'wan, go back to sleep."

He tried to convince her, but it was no use. Suddenly the rooster crowed again and she sat up in bed.

"There ye are. There ye are. See, am I lyin'?" said the brother-in-law. "Ye hear it ye're-self, don't ye?"

His wife crossed herself and said, "Glory be to God. He's

come back to haunt us. Oh, what'll we do, what'll we do?"

"I'm goin' to go right down agin and if I have to kill ivery wan of thim darned fowl I'll get to the bottom av this," and away he went.

He went straight to the coop once more, opened the door and going inside, closed the door after him. He put his flashlight out and waited.

Suddenly the "Cock-a-doodle-do" came again and he put the light on, and what did he see? He couldn't believe his eyes, ONE OF THE CHICKENS was crowing. "Oh," said he, "That's it, is it?" He took his handkerchief off his back pocket and, tying it around the legs of the culprit, slammed the door. When he reached his wife he told her that he had solved the situation and explained what he had discovered.

He killed the chicken the next evening when he came home from work. And a peculiar thing about it was, that when he cleaned it, he discovered (whether it had anything to do with the crowing or not, or maybe the chicken was a morphodite) right through the gizzard was a nail about three inches long. Figure it out for yourself. However, he got his sleep after that— and that ends the story.

To this story, Mr. Fitzpatrick adds: "With the exception that, upon several inquiries afterwards, it was found to be a common occurrence that chickens DO sometimes crow.

"The wife's mother, when told of the occurrence, confirmed this and remarked that there was a four-line poem that was heard frequently in Ireland, apropos of this phenomenon, that went something like this:

"A whistling woman,
"Or crowing hen;
"Is very unlucky
"To single men."

Jack and the House of the Spirits

Now for our promised "Jack tale."

Jack tales, as you know, are always about a young man named Jack who goes out to seek his fortune, falls in with dangerous characters, and escapes by outwitting his enemies. The most famous Jack tale, of course, is "Jack and the Beanstalk." The following one is not so famous, but no less interesting. Considering the impossible situation that Jack finds himself in here, I suspect that this particular story can be traced all the way back to Germany. I also suspect that this yarn, considering its conclusion, was scripted by someone with strong religious convictions.

There was once a young lad named Jack who lived with his widowed mother in a cabin deep in the woods. They were poor and barely had enough food to eat. One day Jack told his mother that he would go off into the world and seek his fortune. Then, when he became a rich man, he would return and share his wealth with her. He swore that they would never want for anything else again.

Jack's mother gave her son her blessing. Then she packed him a change of clothes, some personal items, a little food, and her own personal Bible. These she placed in a sack which he slung over his shoulder. It had snowed the night before, so Jack wore his warm coat and boots. Finally, when he was ready, his mother kissed him and watched as he disappeared into the forest.

Jack journeyed in knee-deep snow all day. It was very cold, and not even his coat afforded enough protection against the chill. Even his feet became numb. By the time night fell he was chilled to the bone and was glad to start a fire. Then he nestled beneath the branches of a big pine tree and ate one of the bannocks that his mother had packed. Afterwards, he pulled his ragged blanket tightly around himself and prepared to go to sleep.

Toward midnight, Jack was awakened by a bright light shining off in the forest. At first he thought it might be someone walking through the woods carrying a lantern. But as he watched, he noticed that the light was not swinging to and fro like a lantern would. Instead the light was standing stone still. *Curious*, he thought to himself. *What kind of light could that be?*

Slowly Jack stood up. The light was slowly approaching. He began to feel pangs of fear. Now he realized that the light had no natural source. He was afraid, yet he was strangely drawn. He walked down a snowy bank and stood by the edge of a little creek. Finally the light stopped and hovered in front of him, about five feet above the ground.

Then a voice said, "Don't be afraid. You are cold. You would like to get warm. And you would like some good food to eat. Follow me and I will show you a house where your every wish can be fulfilled."

The voice was coming out of the light! Jack could hardly believe his ears. His first thought was to run away, but he could only move forward toward the light. The light began to move away as if leading him.

Jack followed the light for the better part of half an hour. Finally he came out of the woods and into a little clearing. The light vanished and Jack saw a little house about three hundred yards away. A weak glow shone through the single window in the front of the house, and a wisp of smoke rose from the chimney. Jack was chilled to the bone and was far away from his camp and his fire. Perhaps the person living in this house was a kind soul who would offer him hot food

and some warmth.

As he approached the house, he noticed that the front door was standing wide open. Inside, sitting in front of the fire, was an old woman. She was stirring something in a big iron pot. Just as he reached the door, the old woman turned toward him.

"Come in, young Jack," she said cheerily. "Come in and warm yourself."

"How do you know my name?" he asked as he stepped through the door.

"I know everything," the old woman replied. "I even know the names of every animal in the forest. I know the names of every tree, every rock, and every brook. Now come in, close the door, and warm yourself by my fire. I have a bowl of piping hot stew for you to eat."

Jack couldn't believe his good luck at finding the hospitable old woman and the cozy, warm house. Suddenly he realized the truth was that he didn't find it by himself. The mysterious light had led him to it. Why? What was going on?

"Come sit by me," the old woman said as she ladled a heaping portion of stew from the iron pot into a wooden bowl. Then she handed the steaming food to Jack who had just seated himself by the fire. The stew smelled delicious.

"Thank you," he said, smiling at the old woman. Then he noticed that she had not dipped out any of the food for herself. "Aren't you going to join me?" he asked.

"No," she replied. "I ate earlier this evening. I am not hungry. But please, young Jack, you eat hearty. You may have as much as you want."

Jack dipped his spoon into the steaming bowl and tasted a bit of the stew. It was the best that he had ever eaten. The old woman smiled at him, and he quickly ate the rest of the stew. Then he held out the bowl for more. The woman quickly obliged.

The combination of the warm fire and the good food made Jack sleepy, and it was not long before he had stretched himself out on the floor. The next thing he knew, it was morning. The snow had stopped, the sky had cleared, and sunlight streamed through the window. At first Jack didn't know where he was, but he soon remembered the cabin in the woods, the kind old woman, and the hot stew. He tried to get up but found that he couldn't move. He was tied hand and foot!

Panicked, he looked around for the old woman. She sat in a corner of the cabin, spinning.

"What are you doing to me?" he asked her. "Why am I all

tied up like this?"

The old woman stopped her spinning and creaked into a standing position. Then she slowly walked toward Jack. "Did you have a good night's sleep, young Jack?" she cackled.

"I asked you," Jack repeated, "why am I all tied up like this?"

"Oh, that," the old woman answered. "I tied you up myself. It took most of the rope that I had in the house, but I tied you up good."

"Why?"

"Now that I have you, I didn't want you to get away—at least until we have had a chance to talk."

"Where am I?" Jack asked. "What is this place?"

"You are in my house," the old woman answered. "This is the house of the spirits. This is a house that is filled with ghosts. Many folks are afraid to come here. It was one of my ghosts, in fact, that led you to me last night."

Jack suddenly remembered the mysterious light in the woods and the voice that came out of it, beckoning him to follow it. Then he found himself standing at the old woman's door. He went inside, sat by the fire, ate some stew, and....

"You poisoned me!" Jack declared. "You are a witch!"

"Some say that I am. Who do you say that I am, young Jack."

"A witch."

"Well," the old woman said, smiling, "I reckon that makes it unanimous."

"Now answer me," Jack demanded, "why am I tied up. I have no money, so there is no use to rob me."

"I know that," the old woman said. "It is I who have the money and I want to give it to you, Jack—all of it. I have much treasure buried out in the woods. I have had it for many years. Now I want to give it to you."

Jack was understandably suspicious. "Why," he said, "are you so generous? And why am I all tied up?"

"Because," the old woman said, "we have to bargain. In order for you to get my treasure you have to do something for me in return. I want you to marry my daughter."

"You have a daughter?" Jack exclaimed. He could hardly imagine a woman so old having a daughter that was yet unmarried.

"Indeed I do," she answered. "She is waiting outside the cabin door at this very moment, anxious to meet you. All I need is your consent."

"Let me see her first," Jack said.

"No," the old woman answered. "I want your consent before she comes in."

"Why can't I see her first?" Jack asked.

"You'll find out soon enough," the old woman cackled.

"And what will happen to me if I refuse? Will you untie me and let me go on my way?"

"Not very likely," she shot back. "You see, the spirits in my house are the souls of those in the past who have refused to marry my daughter. If you refuse, you will join them. If you consent, you will get both a wife and my treasure. You will have enough money to let you live like a king for the rest of your life."

Jack thought for a moment. "I don't see where I have much of a choice."

The old woman smiled. "A very smart decision, young Jack. Does that mean that you consent?"

"As I said, I don't have much of a choice."

"You promise you will not try to run away if I let you loose? I will send my spirits after you if you do. You cannot escape me."

"My word is good."

"Very well," the old woman said as she untied Jack from his bonds. His joints were stiff as he struggled to his feet. In fact he had a somewhat difficult time in keeping his feet at first. Finally he regained his equilibrium. By this time the old woman was standing at the front door. "Young Jack," she said, "I would like you to meet Bernice."

The old woman opened the door, and there on the stoop stood a hunched up figure in a long black dress. She slowly raised her head to show her face. Bernice was an exact copy of the old woman. Jack could not believe his eyes. She was old and wrinkled. She smiled at him and didn't have a tooth in her poor old head.

Bernice shuffled through the doorway, walked over to where Jack was standing, and took his hand. Hers felt cold, like that of a corpse. She smiled up at him again. Jack turned to the old woman.

"This is not your daughter," he said. "This is your sister!"

"My twin sister, to be exact," the old woman snickered.

Jack's eyes filled with righteous indignation. "You lied to me!"

"Come now, Jack. How could you believe that a person who deceived you to begin with could be trusted afterward? You are either the most naive person in the world or the dumbest."

Jack took a deep breath. "Very well," he said with a sigh. "You win."

"Now," the old woman said, "that's much better. I'm sure that you and Bernice will be very happy together."

"I suppose the treasure that you promised is a lie, too?"

"Absolutely. As they say, once a liar always a liar. As for myself, I'm perfectly content to live here alone with my spirits. But Bernice, here, needs someone."

Bernice turned to Jack and smiled her toothless grin.

"She doesn't say much, does she?" Jack asked the old woman.

"No. She was born without a voice."

"Well, that's something at least."

Jack took another deep breath. Then he said, "I left my sack back there by the creek when your spirit brought me here. There are some personal items in there that mean a lot to me. I wonder if I might go get it?"

The old woman looked at Jack, a suspicious bent in her eye. "Are you looking to run away, young Jack?"

"No ma'am. Unlike you, I am a person of my word. I'll be back."

"It's just the sack that you're wantin', is it?"

"Yes, ma'am."

"All right. But I'm warning you. You'd better not try to run, because I'll catch up to you. Then I'll turn you into a spirit, just like those who live with me in my house."

"Yes, ma'am."

"Just to make sure, I'll send one of my spirits with you—just to make sure you don't get eaten by some wild animal." The old woman walked to the front door of the cabin and opened it. "Go on with you, and be back soon—or else!"

Jack had not walked a hundred feet from the house when he felt something at his back. He glanced around and saw an indistinct shadow following him. *That must be the spirit that the old woman said that she would send*, he thought to himself. He walked a little farther and looked again. The shadow was still there, hovering just a little above the ground. When Jack stopped, it stopped. When Jack moved forward, it moved forward.

A half hour later Jack reached the little stream where he had first seen the light. From there it was only a short distance to the big pine tree where he had bedded down the night before. Sure enough, his sack was still under the tree, now partially covered with snow. He picked up his blanket and shook it out. Then he stuffed it into his sack.

Jack looked around. The shadow was still there, hovering twenty feet away. Jack smiled to himself and threw the sack over his back. Then he and the shadow spirit began their return trip to the old woman's cabin.

When he arrived at the door, it was shut. He stopped for a moment and looked for the shadow spirit. It was gone. Maybe it was already inside. He hoped so.

The old woman and her twin sister—Jack's future bride—stood at the front window watching him. Jack shrugged his shoulders and moved toward the door. Suddenly he dropped his sack to the ground and reached inside. Before the two old hags had a chance to move, he pulled out his mother's tattered Bible and put it down on the stoop, jamming it up against the door, making certain that it was in contact with the house. Then he jumped back.

The old woman's eyes widened in horror as she looked out the window. "Get that horrible thing out of there!" she screamed from inside the house.

"Why?" Jack shouted from outside. "It's only my mother's Bible. Surely you can't be afraid of that."

Jack heard a scrambling from inside the house. Then the front door began shaking like someone was trying to get out. But the door wouldn't budge. The old woman's face appeared once again at the window. "Jack, have mercy. Get that thing out of here. We're trapped in the house as long as it sits there touching the house."

"Nothing doing," Jack shot back. "It's going to stay there until you rot!"

"I'll send my spirit out to destroy you."

"I don't think so," Jack replied calmly. "I'm sure that they're trapped in there with you. In fact, I think as long as this Bible remains in place, the countryside will be safe from all of you. And I'm going to make sure that it does stay there!"

Searching around the cabin and outbuildings, Jack found some long iron nails. Then he picked up a large rock. Hurrying back to the front door, Jack drove the nails through the old Bible and fastened it securely to the stoop. Then he stood up and admired his handiwork. The old woman and her sister continued to peer out the front window, looks of abject horror on their faces. They knew that they were trapped in the house—forever—as long at that Bible was there.

"See you around," Jack said to the women as he slung his sack over his shoulder, turned away from the house of the spirits, and sauntered off into the snowy woods.

To this day, parts of that old cabin still stand in the woods. And, people say, fragments of an old Bible are still nailed securely to the front stoop. As long as even a shred remains, the spirits will remain trapped inside. Pity the unfortunate person who would ever remove it.

As for Jack, he returned home and told his mother what had happened. Then he apologized for not bringing home treasure.

"But you did bring home treasure," she told him.

"What are you talking about, Mother?" he asked. "The old woman lied to me about the treasure, just like she lied to me about everything else."

"That's just the point," his mother said. "Through her lies you discovered the most valuable treasure of all—the truth!"

The Silver Bullet

The following is a well-known folktale, and I have heard a number of versions. But I think the best version of all comes from Simeon B. Coffee of Hamblen County, who told the story to the great folklorist and ballad collector John Jacob Niles in May 1934. Niles printed the tale in his book The Ballad Book of John Jacob Niles *(1960 Houghton Mifflin Company). The original version of this magical, yet tragic, story had no title.*

It seems that sometime around the turn of the century a young man lived not far from Witt [Whitwell?], Tennessee—a young man who farmed a reasonably fertile piece of land and supported himself and his widowed mother. His barns bulged with hay and his cribs were filled with shucked corn, and his cows waded in deep pasture grass. This young man (his name was Yancy) and his mother lived well.

During the summer of that year there had been a protracted camp meeting at Bear's Lick Spring Church. It was at this camp meeting that our young Mr. Yancy met a bright-eyed, pink-cheeked girl, of whom he became enamored. Sarah lived just over the top of the hill. Twenty minutes of reasonable walking took him to her door.

As Indian summer came, Yancy's visits to Sarah's home became more frequent and his mother worried for fear her son should marry up with this woman-person and bring her home to the comfortable farmhouse, and bring complications with her. It was in early October when Yancy had his first encounter with a great antlered deer that blocked the path to Miss Sarah's house. At the first encounter, Yancy went home. But when on his next visit the deer once more blocked his path, Yancy, who had provided himself with a rifle, shot

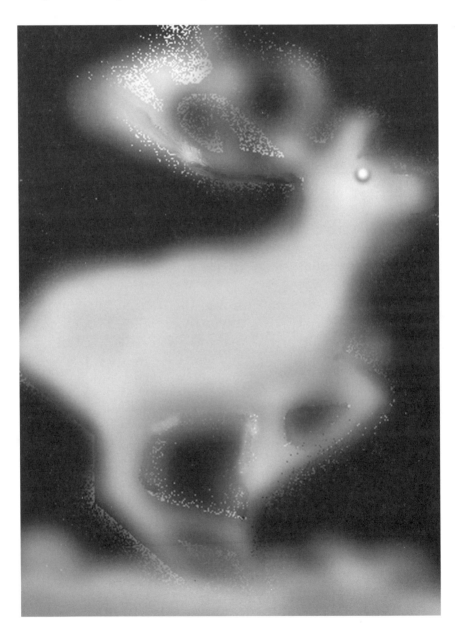

at the deer. The shooting, as he saw it, would serve two purposes—it would rid him of a nuisance and supply him with venison. But no matter how often Yancy fired, he was unable to kill the deer.

With the approach of cold weather, the cattle and hog buyers came through the country, and it was one of these worldly-wise men who advised Yancy on how to destroy the deer—he was to melt down a silver coin and fire it point-blank into the deer's heart. This was the sure and only way.

The following day Yancy melted down a silver dollar, molded it into a bullet, and when next he met the deer and fired the bullet into the animal's heart, the deer fell dead.

Yancy went on to visit Miss Sarah, proposed marriage to her, was accepted, and with joy in his heart returned home through the dark. When he came to the place where the deer had fallen, no deer lay on the ground. Nor was there any sign of the combat that had taken place. Troubled, Yancy walked on home.

The farmhouse door stood wide open. On the floor lay Yancy's mother, quite dead, with a bullet hole just over her heart. Probing the wound with his pocketknife, Yancy found the silver bullet he had molded.

The Ghost Train

Our last story is not a story at all. Rather it is the celebration of a legend and, some say, its lingering memory.

There was once a narrow gauge railroad called East Tennessee and Western North Carolina Railroad—sometimes called the "Tweetsie" or the "Blue Ridge Stemwinder." The ET&WNC was also called by some of the local wags the "Eat Taters and Wear No Clothes."

She ran from Johnson City, Tennessee, to Cranberry, North Carolina. She carried passengers, freight, and the mail. She was the first railroad to cross the Blue Ridge. Until the Tweetsie came to town, folks said the only way to get to Boone, North Carolina, was to be born there.

Generations of passengers rode her swaying cars, going from one place to the other. She took them on excursions. She took them to religious revivals. She took thousands of vacationers to Roan Mountain where they could visit the famous Cloudland Hotel for rest and relaxation.

She was the heartbeat and the soul of East Tennessee and Western North Carolina.

But eventually economics caught up with her. The Tweetsie stopped running in 1950. Most of the old tracks are now rusted or were torn up and sold for scrap. The passengers and freight cars are now scattered across the country. One of the old engines, however, is still in service hauling ore from a mine in Colorado.

Today, just outside Blowing Rock, North Carolina, there is Tweetsie Railroad Park where, for an admission, you are able to ride a small section of the Tweetsie and get held up by desperadoes and attacked by Indians—something you would never have experienced while the railroad was in operation.

But those who believe that even old railroad locomotives—especially legendary ones—have a life after death need only to stand by a section of Tweetsie track in Elizabethton in the wee small hours of the morning. If you listen carefully and keep your eyes peeled, you just might see the shadow of a legend coming down that track toward you—a ghostly locomotive, puffing smoke and blowing steam.

Yes, there are those who have actually seen the ghost train. In a state filled with ghostly legends, who would deny the possibility of the ghost of a legendary railroad that chugs up a ghostly track, past an old station, and roars off into the night?

Also available from your
local bookstore or
The Overmountain Press

Haunted Tennessee

by
Charles Edwin Price

From the hills and valleys of the Appalachian Mountains to the winding course of the broad Mississippi River, Tennessee is a haunted state. During its bicentennial year, Tennesseans will be reflecting on their heritage, and ghost tales are very much a part of that. Adults and children alike will enjoy the stories, superstitions, and traditions that have been included in this collection.

The sound of a steam locomotive rumbles down the hallway of Tennessee High School, causing students to run for cover... A lone woman confronts the infamous Bell Witch of Tennessee in her bedroom... A murderous hobo haunts an Erwin graveyard in the dark of night, terrifying everyone who sees him... A strange rock from the foundation of a medieval monastery haunts a wealthy Murfreesboro man... In Fentress County, a long lost child's footprints once more go on for miles in new snow, and in the West Tennessee town of Dyersburg another child returns from the grave for one last hug from her father...

And what about the "King of Rock and Roll?" Is Elvis still alive, or is it his ghost that pops up in the oddest places?

These are but a few of the haunting tales from the Volunteer State that have been included in this volume.